COLLECTING

Crackle le

Glass

WITH VALUES

Judy H. Alford

Photography by Paul Gilmore

Schiffer Publishing Ltd

77 Lower Valley Road, Atglen, PA 19310

Dedication

It was not very difficult to choose the one I would like to dedicate this book to because there is only one who is primarily responsible for my interest in crackle glass...my husband, Claude L. Alford, Jr. Since before Claude and I were married we shared a love of this precious glass. We've spent hundreds of hours together...looking at and studying crackle glass. His knowledge of this glass was far greater than mine, yet he shared it all with me to make this book possible. I dedicate this book to you, Claude, because of your unselfish love for me and your dream to see me publish this book on crackle glass.

Copyright © 1997 by Judy Alford
Library of Congress Catalog Card Number: 96-72029

Designed by "Sue"

Printed in China
ISBN: 0-7643-0217-5

Published by Schiffer Publishing Ltd.
77 Lower Valley Road
Atglen, PA 19310
Phone: (610) 593-1777; Fax: (610) 593-2002
E-mail: schifferbk@aol.com

Please write for a free catalog.
This book may be purchased from the publisher.
Please include $2.95 for shipping.
Try your bookstore first.

We are interested in hearing from authors
with book ideas on related subjects.

Table of Contents

Acknowledgments

First of all I would like to thank my family—Claude, my husband, and Justin and Danielle, my children—for the support they have given me through the last year. They have all been great and have eaten a lot of sandwiches and microwaveables without complaint. I couldn't have made it without their support and encouragement.

Danielle, my dear daughter...who is twelve, started me off with the right equipment. She put together a briefcase full of everything I needed to write this book...and Justin, my fifteen-year old son, I thank you for your interest, your ideas, and your encouragement. It meant so much to your mom.

Justin...here's to your friend, Michael Jordan, who sat with me at my kitchen table while I worked on my book with words of encouragement. Thanks, Michael.

To Dr. Brenda Manning, my sister, who has written several educational books and who acts like it's no big deal, I say thank you for being a role model I desire to mimic.

To my baby sister, Kim Turner, whose steadfast love and encouragement lifts my spirits...thanks for always being there for me, Kim. You will never know what your confidence and encouragement have meant to me.

To Gerry Gossett, my guardian angel, whose encouragement and never wavering confidence in me reached my soul and brought out talents in me I never knew existed...but Gerry did. Thanks, Gerry.

To my two closest friends, Joyce O'Barr and Mary George Jester, whom I have leaned on and used for my sounding boards more times than I can count...I say thanks. Mary George, I appreciate the push at just the right time, and Joyce, thanks for your genuine confidence in me. I love you both and cherish your friendships.

For all those who worked with me and let me steal precious time from them and their families, I thank you. Donald and Jane Thompson, who have been so willing to share their hundreds of pieces of precious crackle glass with me, as well as sharing their knowledge of this glass...I am most appreciative.

To those who have loaned me their prized possessions to be photographed: Candace Alford Reid, my stepdaughter; Kelly Brown, my niece; Lucille Holcomb, my mother; Danielle Howle, my daughter; Brenda Manning, my sister; Dana Noggle, Donald and Jane's daughter; and Pat Paschall, my sister-in-law, who also gave me the use of two most helpful books...for this I am most grateful.

There is one person to whom I owe the success of the completion of this book...my mother, Lucille Holcomb...thanks Mom. Thanks for believing in me and offering your support, both emotional and financial, to make this dream come true. Your continued confidence, steadfast love, and support have seen me through...again.

Mary George Jester...without you I would have never found the time to complete this book. Thank you for hauling three computers across country...kidnapping me from the hustle and bustle of a teen, a preteen, a husband, a wedding, and my baby dachshund...carrying me to the most peaceful slice of heaven in the north Georgia mountains...and demanding completion of this book. Only a true friend would have single-handedly typed the entire text of this book while I wrote and typed the captions. You have my heartfelt gratitude and appreciation. I owe you a big one.

There are so many people I have met during my research that I must thank for helping me gather the information necessary to write this book. Mr. Dean Six, Historian, Author and Collector of West Virginia glass, is the most knowledgeable glass person I know, as well as the busiest. As you will see, he took the time out of his hectic schedule not only to aid me in my research but to write the history preface. I will be forever grateful for his encouragement and enthusiasm for my work and for giving freely his knowledge and hard earned research to be sure history was reported factually. My book would not have been possible without his help.

The owners of the "crackle glass 'since-closed' companies" have been wonderful. My sincere appreciation goes to Mr. and Mrs. Henry Manus, "Mr. and Mrs. Rainbow," who talked with me and wrote me time and again answering the many questions I had about Rainbow and crackle glass. Mr. Rainbow's right arm, Mr. Paul Kilgore, was so helpful and trusted me with his most sentimental possessions...his old Rainbow catalogs...along with much more needed history and other valued information.

Mr. Keith Merritt, for whom I searched so diligently, was great. He let me keep him on the phone for over an hour. He then mailed me a most treasured gift...old Kanawha catalogs...along with much more needed history and other valued information.

I was able to purchase old Bischoff and Pilgrim catalogs, and the wonderful people at Fenton Art Glass Collectors Of America, Inc., out of Williamstown, West Virginia, mailed me the pages out of their catalogs of the few pieces of crackle glass Fenton manufactured in 1992 and 1993. I talked with many helpful people at Blenko, Pilgrim, and Fenton and received all the information I requested for my research. Special thanks goes to Lori and Judy at Pilgrim for going out of their way to assist me. Everyone was wonderful.

Mr. Robert Hamon's help is appreciated in identifying his pieces, and Mr. Paul Kilgore of Rainbow was very gracious to help in the identification of Rainbow pieces. He also mailed me much sought after information about Rainbow and the Viking Glass Company. The Pilgrim office had their glass specialist, Mr. Robert

McKeand, identify the Pilgrim pieces and sent me information on their history and answered my questions time and again. Mr. Charles P. Sloan, who purchased Bischoff, and Mr. Henry Manus, of Rainbow, helped me to understand the crackling process. To all, I give my heartfelt appreciation and thanks, because it took each of you to make this book possible.

I would like to thank the man who took the first 100 crackle glass photographs for me...Billy Moorehead, of the Pacer Studio in Hartwell, Georgia (my hometown). Thanks Billy for such a wonderful job, as always. However, the fear of glass breakage caused me to seek a local photographer...Paul Gilmore of Madison, Georgia. Paul and his wife, Dawn, made numerous trips to my home and set up to photograph hundreds of pieces of crackle glass. Thank you both for making my job so pleasant and a lot less complicated. Your work is outstanding.

There is also another Dawn I would like to mention...my editor, Dawn Stoltzfus. Thanks for your professional guidance, ideas, and most of all for your patience. Everyone at Schiffer Publishing has been godsent. I especially want to thank Peter Schiffer, for his encouragement and the confidence and faith shown by giving me this opportunity to bring you *Collecting Crackle Glass*.

Foreword

My husband's mother left him three pieces of crackle glass. You will see photographs of those pieces in the book, along with many other pieces of antique glass. My husband learned much from his mom, who collected all types of antique glassware, and not only appreciated its beauty but wanted to know about its history. She had much knowledge about crackle glass and other antique glassware and shared it all with her son, who was eager to learn.

After her death, Claude (my husband) and one of his friends, Donald Thompson, examined the pieces of crackle glass Claude's mother left him. They were intrigued by their beauty and began looking for other pieces. Donald and Jane (Donald's wife) and Claude and I would spend hours searching through flea markets, antique shops, garage sales, and antique shows, each trying to outdo the other with the most beautiful and unusual find at the least expense. We also bought crackle glass at antique auctions and estate sales. We paid anywhere from fifty cents to several dollars for a piece of crackle glass the first few years we collected...and up to ninety-five dollars in more recent years.

My husband and I carry on his mother's love for antique glass. On our honeymoon, we pulled a trailer behind our car and drove into four different states in search of antique glass—crackle glass in particular. We gathered every little piece of knowledge we could find about this beautiful glass and came home with over fifty pieces of crackle glass, a greater appreciation for its creator, and an extended knowledge of its history.

Our love for this spectacular glass has already rubbed off on my daughter, Danielle. She loves collecting and can now pick out the most valuable and older pieces all by herself. So, this family has already gone into the third generation of crackle glass collectors. We have been collecting crackle glass for approximately seven years. Together with Donald and Jane, our collections total about 600 pieces. You will see I have used many of Donald and Jane's pieces, and we have enjoyed looking at each piece and reminiscing about our fun finding each one.

We never could understand why there was so little written information about this gorgeous glassware. Ev-

ery once in a while, we would gather some new and interesting information; however, we were never satisfied that such little attention was given to such "beautiful glass" and "creative talents."

When my husband opened his antique shop (Oconee Antiques) in Buckhead, Georgia, I noticed there were many collectors of this unique glassware. The collectors would ask us if any written information was available about crackle glass. "None that we know of," was our standard answer. I decided to do something about that.

My research was both informative and exciting as I talked with owners, presidents, and employees of all the major crackle glass producers. Companies that have been closed for many years came alive again as the stories were told. These stories, along with much printed information from these companies, were obtained along with old company catalogs and other original brochures and advertisements. It was so exciting for me to open an old company catalog and see on the pages the actual pieces displayed in my collection, and it was even more exciting to be able to talk with the people who were responsible for the birth of this spectacular glassware. I will treasure these conversations in my memories and value each piece of history I have collected from the company owners, glass blowers, plant managers and other experts in this field from across the United States.

I've learned much in my research; however, some knowledge can't be learned in books or through research. Studying the glass itself is extremely important. I have handled, looked at, felt and studied age marks, styles, handles, colors, weights, textures, and the creativity of literally thousands of pieces of crackle glass.

This book begins with a walk through a manufacturing plant from yesteryear which will help the reader understand the hand blowing and crackling procedures used when giving birth to a piece of crackle glass.

Another major area of concern to collectors is having the ability to distinguish old crackle glass from new, since crackle is still being manufactured by some of the original companies, as well as being imported from foreign countries. I will discuss ways of identifying old glass and the procedure to take in determining the approximate age of each piece. I will show new pieces made in Taiwan, China, and Japan, and briefly discuss how to spot the reproduced pieces.

I will discuss the pricing of crackle glass based on the most collectible guidelines giving collectors an advantage when shopping for additions to their collections. These guidelines list the five most collectible categories. Each of these areas will elevate the value of a purchase and is important information for collectors and dealers alike.

In Chapter One I will give a "beginner's lesson" on getting to know crackle glass using picture illustrations. Chapter Two will illustrate the five most collectible categories, giving identification information. The five areas that will be covered are 1) Colors: A. Most expensive colors to produce and B. Rare and unusual colors; 2) Shapes: A. Rare and unusual shapes and B. Oversized pieces; 3) Stoppered Pieces; 4) Identified Pieces: A. Marked, B. Labeled, and C. Number; and 5) Signed Pieces.

In Chapter Three I've given information to identify some of the 1853-1930 companies that manufacture crackle glass and the type of pieces they produced. A summary sheet will follow. Some background information about the crackle glass companies that only produced a small quantity of crackle glass (1930-1940) is given for those who would like to dig a little deeper into their history.

Chapter Four is divided by the *major* producers of crackle glass, giving their history and illustrations of their "most plentiful shapes and colors" of art. A Manufacturer's Identification Guide for the 1930-1990 major companies is furnished to assist you in identifying the manufacturers of most pieces found today—West Virginia Crackle.

Chapter Five will give illustrated pictures of Specialty Collections:1) Kitchen and Household Collecting and 2) Perfume Bottle Collecting.

I am extremely excited about this book and the information it furnishes. There were over 450 colored photographs of crackle glass illustrated, and only a very few pieces were left without a positive identification of their maker. We now have a great start! However, there is always more to be learned about this unique type of art and its creators. I have been extremely careful to identify the manufacturer, age, and price each specimen as accurately as possible according to the information available. If errors are found and new information is mailed to me, the correction will be made in any updated reprints in the future.

I am constantly searching for new information on crackle glass, and if anyone has access to any new information on this subject or can name the manufacturer of any unidentified piece of crackle glass in this book, please make me aware of it by writing to Judy Alford, 1210 Alford Lane, Buckhead, Georgia 30625. I hope that the next updated issue can be as full of new and exciting information about crackle glass as this one is.

West Virginia Crackle Glass Manufacturers 1930-1970

In the 1978 edition of *The World Book Dictionary*, crackling is defined, figuratively, as being "brilliant; lively; and sparkling." Crackle glass is a very unique piece of artwork. Each piece has individuality, character, and personality all its own. This is one reason I never tire of examining each specimen so carefully—one can always find interesting and new detail with each inspection.

Unlike the earlier years when manufacturing companies were scattered all across the United States, producers of crackle glass in the later years settled in West Virginia. These West Virginia companies are primarily the source of all crackle glass found today. There were approximately twenty to thirty glass companies that produced crackle glass during the 1930-1970 years. The major producers of crackle glass during these years were Bischoff, Blenko, Kanawha/Hamon, Pilgrim, and Rainbow. All of these companies were West Virginia companies.

These particular companies are the ones on which I chose to do extensive research. I also included Fenton in this research because of their popularity. Fenton did not produce any crackle glass in the 1930-1970 years but did produce crackle glass in the 1992 and 1993 years. Imperial, also a very popular company out of Bellaire, Ohio, experimented with crackle glass using some of their candlewick pieces but never put it on the line. So, if you find a piece of candlewick and it is crackled, you have an extremely valuable piece of glass.

There are other companies that produced crackle glass during these years: Williamsburg (owned by Kanawha and used Kanawha molds, produced very few crackle glass pieces during the early 1970s), Heritage, Cober, Moncer, Voglesong, Spring Valley, Gill, Sloan, Tri-State, Viking, Weston, Bonita, Bruce & Emch, West Virginia Glass Specialty Company, and Moreland. There may be others that I have not discovered yet but I believe I have covered the vast majority of the companies that produced crackle glass and give as little or as much information about each of these companies as I found available. I am hopeful this information will be helpful to others when researching these companies further.

Preface: West Virginia Crackle Glass History
by Dean Six

Crackle or craquelle glass has been produced for a very long time. The earliest references to crackle I find is the notation that it appears in the second half of the 16th century in Venetian glass. Apparently both methods of crackle production— dipping the gather of hot glass into water followed by reheating, and the method of rolling the hot gather in small chips of broken glass—were employed quite early. While we may think of crackle glass in terms of 20th century collectible glass, it is recorded that "Crackle glass was particularly popular in the North (of Italy), especially in Liege in the 17th century." (*Three Great Centuries of Venetian Glass: A Special Exhibit 1958.* Corning Museum of Glass.) Bohemian craftsmen copied crackle effects and the processes were spread across Europe.

In the English classic *Curiosities of Glass Making*, Apsely Pellatt describes and illustrates, with step-by-step drawings, how to craft crackle glass. He called it "Venetian Frosted Glass" and produced crackle as early as the mid 1840s.

American crackle glass is noted at an early date in trade journal references and advertisements of Hobbs, Brockunier & Co., of Wheeling, West Virginia. As early as October 1882 the China & Glass Journal mention "crackled ware first made in this section by this firm is becoming more and more popular." Their immense production ability had at this time already embraced "art glass." Hobbs marketed their product as "craquelle" in several colors, including ruby, canary, and blue. (*Hobbs, Brockunier & Co., Glass.*, Neila and Tom Bredehoft. Collectors Books) Other American glass houses, such as the Boston and Sandwich Glass Works, were producing crackle by the 1800s. A circa 1874 Boston and Sandwich Glass catalogue illustrates some thirty-nine shapes in crackle or overshot, the process of making glass "frosted," as the catalogue describes it, by the rolling of hot glass in small broken glass pieces to create the effect. This glass is rough to the touch and lacks the "broken" look of most 20th century crackle. (*The Acorn Volume III*, 1992. Sandwich Glass Museum). Today collectors generally differentiate between the two types of glass once called crackle—"craquelle" being the type rolled in glass chips

overshot glass. It seems it was all called crackle glass at the time of its manufacture.

When I began to look for an explanation as to why 20th century American crackle glass production was largely centered in West Virginia, and more specifically around Huntington and up the Teays River Valley in West Virginia, I found no real answer.

After a decade of sleuthing, researching glass factory histories and "genealogies" of the flow of skilled workers, I offer this well researched theory. Please do not lose sight of the fact that this is only at this time a theory offered as explanation. All the facts, the components of the theory, are accurate and verifiable. I take responsibility for the connecting assumptions and offer them only as possibility for your consideration at this time.

The question that precedes why crackle glass was produced in West Virginia is why was so much glass produced in West Virginia?

Since around 1815 glass has been produced in what is now West Virginia because of three predominate reasons: natural resources, transportation, and skilled labor.

It was coal that attracted glass manufacturers to the hills. And years later when changing technology replaced coal with more efficient natural gas, West Virginia was found to have great storehouses of that as well. Whatever the heat source, the largest ingredient in a glass batch (recipe) is sand. Sand was available nearby of a quality that produced good glass, or if shipped from nearby, transportation was not an obstacle. Transportation was an early inducement to glass in this region. The Ohio river was "the way west" and west was where people were moving. Wheeling (and Pittsburgh) were glass centers for supplying the west. When river travel dimmed, the same railroad networks that had been developed for coal and timber, both rich resources in West Virginia, could carry finished glass out by the railroad car full, and they did.

The last component is skilled labor. Glass requires varied skill levels, some are high skilled and the skill is passed on by an apprenticeship-like system. Skilled labor was a significant positive factor in seeding additional glass company ventures where a glass worker's community developed the ability to draw on such resources, to lure workers from one factory to another.

These factors combined account largely for the presence of glass factories in great number being in West Virginia. Other states also had large glass industries, but none seem to have had the concentration of crackle glass. Why? To this end I offer my theory and research notes.

Much of the glass produced in the region of Huntington and Teays River Valley of West Virginia has a set of regional characteristics. This area's glass is frequently mouth blown and hand crafted or shaped, not pressed, and infrequently blown into a patterned mold. It often has a pontil mark, left rough or polished to a smooth recessed disk. Pontil marks are those scars, usually on the bottom of a object, remaining from when an iron rod or "pontil" was attached to hold the object while it was manipulated and shaped still hot.

The area's glass often incorporates one or more of the hand formed glass techniques of:

Spatter, the inclusion of small differently colored glass chips into the object's surface when the object is being formed,

Rigaree, the application of a trail or heavy thread of additional glass on the surface of an object,

Applied Embellishment, in the forms of differently colored feet and handles on objects but more dramatically glass applied as knops or finials on lids, applied leaves, applied prunts or other "laid and fused on the surface while hot treatments." Prunts are small seals of hot glass with points, bumps or design on the surface of the seal. All of these are fairly common in glass from this area, along with *crackle* effects.

What is striking is that any of these techniques are uncommon in the larger picture of glass production. In the several hundred glass factories that have existed in West Virginia such techniques are very uncommon. However, in the roughly twenty glass tableware and decorative glass factories in the Huntington-Teays Valley area at least thirteen used some combination (or all) of these techniques! What is uncommon to rare elsewhere is a common practice in this very limited area. What is the common thread? The techniques may stem from the glass giant mentioned above, Hobbs, Brockunier and Co. in Wheeling decades earlier.

Many glass creators and factory visionaries who were later successful or shaped some part of the glass industry had their start at Hobbs. Michael Owens is just one example; he invented the bottle machine and revolutionized glass making. Owens began his glass career at Hobbs.

An amazing host of glass pioneers began their careers or worked early in life at Hobbs. They had acquired skill, launched careers, and somehow become excited about the opportunities glass offers while at Hobbs. But the real connection between earlier American crackle glass and the cluster of 20th century crackle producers around Huntington-Teays Valley may be one man—Otto Jaeger.

Born in Germany, he came to America at around age thirteen, and by age twenty-four had come to Wheeling to "take charge of the engraving and other departments of the Hobbs, Brockuiner glass plant." Jaeger left Hobbs to become one of the organizers of Fostoria Glass Co, was later the founding president of Seneca Glass Co., and by 1901 had returned to Wheeling to found Bonita Art Glass Co. Bonita was a decorator and producer of glass. Around 1925 Jaeger and Bonita Glass had relocated to Huntington, West Virginia.

At Bonita, Jaeger was said in glass trade journals to be making glass in the tradition that Hobbs had used years earlier. Mentioned are certain art glass types, including crackle. This direct reference to the Hobbs legacy carries to Huntington a skill and knowledge that ties 20th century crackle in West Virginia to the earliest craquelle made at Hobbs. The thread and common link is Otto Jaeger. Perhaps he had with him skilled glass artisans or old friends who were the teachers of others, whatever the details we may never know. But Jaeger seems the missing link.

Examples of paper labeled Bonita Glass illustrates the use of *all* of the techniques ascribed above as regional characteristics for the Huntington-Teays Valley glass houses.

It appears Otto Jaeger was the pioneer, the carrier of the technical know-how, and the marketing visionary who supplanted crackle glass, and likely other related techniques to the Huntington-Teays Valley. As he and others who had been educated at Hobbs and carried those skills and techniques across the United States, glass crafters who were trained at Hobbs followed a centuries old pattern of becoming independent with their skills, replicating the processes and forms they knew with their own variations and additions, and perpetuating a technique. I suggest to you that West Virginia, rich in the resources to make glass, became a mid-20th century crackle production center because it followed the old pattern: learn the skill, perfect the skill, leave the original factory, begin a new factory, duplicate what you know and try to expand on it to create new (but always somehow reflective of its origins) glass.

—Dean Six
Historian, Author, and Collector

Dean Six is a major part of the mission of the West Virginia Museum of American Glass, Ltd., whose goal is to organize and promote a centralized glass museum in West Virginia. They are gathering glass history about all types of glass makers and hope to exhibit and interpret not just "collectible glass," but as many facets of glass as possible.

Dean Six is in the process of putting together *The Index to Dean Six's Encyclopedia of West Virginia Glass*. The "master" volume has been a work in progress of over five years. It is almost 500 pages in length and growing. He hopes to complete this index by the year 2000. The book will be an index to every "glass manufacturer" that ever made West Virginia their home since around 1815, what type glass they produced, and the years they operated in West Virginia. What an undertaking!

1. Getting to Know Crackle Glass

Creating a Piece of Crackle Glass

At least four thousand years ago, perhaps on the sands of Egypt, Syria, or Babylon, someone discovered how to make glass. Since that ancient day, humankind has fostered this knowledge as a sacred heritage from generation to generation. For many years now, the skill of the glass worker has been a source of beauty to be treasured by all people.

In *Blenko Glass, 1930-1953*, by Eason Eige and Rick Wilson, a scripture verse is mentioned which touches on the value of glass in a discussion about the worth of "wisdom," found in the book of Job 28:17. Quoting from the King James Version, it reads: "The gold and the crystal cannot equal it: and the exchange of it shall not be for jewels of fine gold." So, glass or crystal was ranked right up there with gold and jewels. Making glassware by hand is the oldest industry in America, having been originated in the Jamestown Colony in 1608.

Glass is truly the product of God-given earth and fire. Let's imagine we are in a manufacturing plant watching a "pretend" piece of crackle glass being produced. To make this valued treasure, you start with silica (sand most often found in the West Virginia quarries), soda ash, lime, and feldspar. Then you add small quantities of various other chemicals to create the color, such as copper, selenium, manganese, cadmium, gold, etc., to make a 2000 pound "batch." After the mixing and screening of select ingredients, a quantity of broken glass called "cutlet" is added to the "batch" to speed up the melting process. The raw materials are now ready to be fused into glass by fire.

The furnace or tank into which the glass worker throws the "batch," shovel by shovel, has been prefixed to a concentrated intense heat of 2700 degrees Fahrenheit. In about eighteen hours, the glass in this tank will be ready to be gathered and blown.

The red glow of fire is everywhere, and through the glow walk the gatherers, bit-boys, handlers, heat-in boys, and carry-in boys, passing the blowpipes and punties with glass from one to the other as each finishes his particular job and proceeds to the next. It takes a shop of six to ten people to complete one piece of art. Glory holes are kept at a temperature hot enough to reheat the tops of the half-finished items. They are built with three openings: North, West, and South. Those openings are enlarged or reduced by the workers, depending on the size of the item.

The blowpipe used in the glass blowing process is a hollow tube of steel with a special "head" which the gatherer dips into the red opening in the tank of molten glass. Turning it around and around, he gathers just the right "gob" of molten glass on the end of the pipe. He hands it to the blower after first rolling it on a "marveling plate," a one-inch thick, fourteen inch wide and two feet long table top stand that tilts at a 45 degree angle, making it easier to roll the glass. The marveling plate is steel, very smooth and from time to time polished with a wax and paste mixture that is also used by most all other workers to keep tools smooth and thus avoid scratches on glasses. The blower then shapes the "ball" with tools, apple wood block and paddle, and with carefully controlled breaths and puffs form a hollow bulb. His tools are varied, adapted for each item, and include the pucellas, often called just the "tool." Like a huge pair of tweezers, the "tool" becomes a set of additional fingers for the skilled glass craftsman. After this, if it is to be applied, another craftsman applies special finishes such as crackle.

Several techniques of crackling glass were used, depending on which company or artist was creating the piece, but each method produced similar results. To obtain crackle this hot piece of glass is dipped in a fifty-five gallon drum of cold water to cause the glass to crack and is then refired to seal these cracks. The temperature of the water and length of time left in the water controls the size of the cracks and the number of fractions in the glass. The movement of the water by a hose connected in a drum helps cause the cracks to be more evenly spread.

Another technique of crackling glass used in earlier years was rolling the hot glass in wet sawdust before dipping it in the cold water. This sawdust served as a protectant for the glass. The cracks in these pieces would be very small and more evenly spread when compared to pieces that were dipped in the cold water without any protection. These unprotected pieces would have much larger crackles that were not as evenly spread. Their texture would be thicker and duller and was sometimes referred to as "alligator" crackle.

Now the piece has been crackled and is ready to be removed from the blowpipe and turned over to the stick-up boy who picks it up by attaching the end of a punty rod to the base of the bulb-shaped piece which he carries to the "glory-hole," a reheating furnace kept about 2500 degrees Fahrenheit. Here the glass becomes hot enough again to be taken to the finisher at his bench for further shaping on top. Now, from the skillful touch of practiced hands, the glass takes on its final form as a decanter, bowl, vase, pitcher, cruet, etc. When the piece is to have rings, handles, etc., applied, it is handed to a second finisher.

As these finishers complete the piece, a carry-in boy appears with a special asbestos-covered fork, snaps the piece from the punty and carries it to an annealing oven, called a "lehr." Here it travels on a slowly moving endless chain through several hours of ever-reducing heat, emerging at the end ready to be picked up by hand and inspected. Our "pretend" piece of crackle glass in now finished.

The glass is then labeled and boxed for shipment to the stores where pieces are purchased and cherished for years to come. Now, if we search long enough and hard enough, we can purchase these very same pieces from antique stores, flea markets, estate sales, etc. When we are lucky enough to find these pieces of treasure, we purchase them and add them to our most prized possessions.

There may have been some variation from these procedures taken to create our "pretend" piece of crackle glass, but basically, they were very similar in all manufacturing plants. These procedures were furnished to me in a red pamphlet called the *Creation of Fine Handblown Glassware by Rainbow* sent to me by Mr. Henry Manus, the former President and owner of the Rainbow Art Glass Co., Inc.

Glass making by hand requires not only skill at a high level, but teamwork that is swift, accurate, and perfectly coordinated. Its basic methods have been unchanged through many centuries. All free form hand-blown glass is shaped by hand, and variations in size, shape, and color are acceptable and lend real individuality to each item. The pontil mark is truly proof of a hand blown piece of artwork and the great talent, creativity, and time which goes into the creation of all hand blown free form pieces.

There are two types of mold blown methods; one that left a side seam and another that did not. Both of these methods, of course, were a little less time consuming than the free form. One type of mold blown which called for turning the piece in the mold left no side seams and would have a pontil mark, as did the free form pieces. The other type mold blown that was not turned would have side seams and no pontil mark. A smooth bottom on a piece would indicate this type mold blown procedure was used, with the exception of some Hamon pieces where applied pontil marks were used to give some of their mold blown pieces the "free form effect."

Manufacturing companies represented L-R: Hamon, Pilgrim, Blenko, Pilgrim, and Unknown.

A display of vibrant colors and exquisite craftsmanship. Manufacturing companies represented L-R: Kanawha, Pilgrim,
Rainbow, Pilgrim, and Kanawha.

Manufacturing companies represented L-R: Rainbow, Pilgrim, Fry, Pilgrim, and Rainbow.

Manufacturing companies represented L-R: Pilgrim, Blenko, Rainbow, Kanawha, Kanawha/Hamon, and Hamon.

Crackle glass is beautiful displayed in an elegant style.

The manufacturer's styles, shapes, and colors of crackle glass vary.

Companies represented L-R: Two Rainbow, probably Blenko, Pilgrim, Blenko, Unknown, Hamon, Viking, and Fry.

Crackle glass also fits in with the country look.

Crackle glass colors differ in shades and colors within each manufacturing company. A variety of amberina colors are represented by L-R: Two Rainbow and two Kanawha.

More variety in the amberina color represented by L-R: Hamon and three Kanawha.

A variety of reds are shown L-R: Pilgrim, Rainbow, Kanawha (apple), two Pilgrim, and Rainbow.

A variety of yellows are shown L-R: Pilgrim, Kanawha, Blenko, and Pilgrim.

A wide variety and variation in shades of colors are shown in this display of green glass L-R: Pilgrim, Bischoff, Rainbow, and three Pilgrims.

More shades of green L-R: Pilgrim, Kanawha, and three Pilgrim.

A variety of blues are shown Front: Pilgrim; Back, L-R: Unknown, Blenko, Pilgrim, Dereume, and Pilgrim.

More shades of blue are shown L-R: Three Pilgrim, probably Rainbow, and Pilgrim.

Crackle glass producers made the same styles but in different sizes as shown in these two ruby red Hamon pieces.

Crackle glass producers made the same styles and shapes in different colors. Represented L-R: Two Rainbow pitchers in ruby red and amber...the amber piece has very fine crackles while the ruby red one has thick alligator crackles.

Crackle glass styles within each company will vary in color. This Pilgrim style is shown in tangerine, ruby red, and olive green.

Some manufacturing companies would produce the same style item in plain glass as well as crackled glass. Represented L-R: A Blenko fish in plain glass (it also came in crackled) and a Blenko vase in crackled glass (it also came in plain glass).

Manufacturing companies represented Front, L-R: Kanawha, Rainbow; Back, L-R: Pilgrim, Kanawha, and Pilgrim.

Manufacturing companies represented Front: Pilgrim; Back, L-R: Rainbow and Kanawha.

A close-up look at crackle glass. Manufacturing companies represented Front, L-R: Two Pilgrim; Back, L-R: Pilgrim, Kanawha.

Manufacturing companies represented Front, L-R: Kanawha, Rainbow, and Kanawha; Back, L-R: Two Blenko.

Represented Fry "crackle" glass (cracks obtained by crackling), Dark amber lemonade pitcher with applied dark green handle and finial on the lid, H. C. Fry Glass Company, 1901-1933, H. 11". Value $125-$175.

Represented Fry "craquel" glass (cracked look obtained from a mold) clear tea pitcher, H. C. Fry Glass Company, 1901-1933, H. 8.5". *Courtesy of Jane and Donald Thompson.* Value $50-$75.

23

My Favorite Glass Pieces

(Top to Bottom, Left to Right:) **Yellow Blenko Vase:** This piece was also found in the *Blenko Glass 1930-1953,* by Eason Eige and Rick Wilson, Copyright 1987, pp. 31, 87. The original price was $1.80. Height 10".

Green Rainbow Decanter With Exquisite Stopper: This piece certainly shows talent in craftsmanship. It is one of the most unusual and beautiful pieces I own. The length of the stopper measures three inches longer than the decanter itself. The stopper measures 9" and the decanter 6". Height 13".

Cranberry Crackled Decanter With Round Crackled Stopper: This piece was bought at a flea market in Augusta, Georgia. It was marked Czechoslovakia. I paid more for this piece than I normally spend on my crackle glass finds because I was intrigued by its beauty. The color is almost iridescent, with a lot of purple and yellow in it. Height 7".

Topaz Fry Glass Lemonade Pitcher With Applied Jade Green Handle And Finial On Lid: This piece was found in *The Antique Trader, Antiques and Collectibles Price Guide, 1988,* pg. 596 in a photograph shown with delft blue accessories. It was common for the H.C. Fry Company to produce jade green and delft blue accessories to a piece. This piece was priced at $160.00. It is one of the oldest pieces I own. The company was in business from 1901-1933 in Rochester, Pennsylvania. Notice the lip of the lid is very deep—this is common in older pieces. Height 11".

Ruby Red #925 Bischoff Pitcher: This piece was found in a Bischoff catalog, 1922-1963. Bishcoff pieces are usually a heavier glass. The majority of our collection, as you will see, is ruby red and amberina. Height 7".

Amberina Rainbow Vase With Applied Red Decorated Neck: This piece has the most sentimental attachment of all...my husband bought it in Dillard, Georgia, at an antique mall on our honeymoon. This was the first piece we bought after we were married. The quality of this glass and the craftsmanship are exquisite. We paid $55 for this piece in 1989. Height 5.5".

Cobalt Blue Blenko Crackled Basket: This is the only dark blue cobalt piece in our collection. It is also one of only two basket pieces we have. The glass is thick, and the crackles are large. We bought this piece at the Jockey Lot in Anderson, South Carolina. The manufacturer appears to be Blenko. Height 7.5".

Companies that are represented in this picture of my favorite pieces of crackle glass. Top: Blenko; Middle, L-R: Rainbow, Unidentified, and Fry; Back, L-R: Bischoff, Rainbow, and Blenko.

Green Blenko crackle glass lamp. This lamp was found in *Blenko Glass 1930-1953,* by Eason Eige and Rick Wilson, copyright 1987, pg. 113. This lamp was introduced in the 1951 catalog. The base sold for $27.50 and the shade for $5.00. H. 32". Value $175-$225.

Determining Approximate Age of Crackle Glass

It is believed that crackle glass was originally made by the Venetians in the sixteenth century, but most of the ware found today dates from the 1800s.

Old crackle is not easily detected, however, I have found that taking a magnifying glass and looking for wear and scratch marks on the bottom of each piece is an effective way of detecting older pieces. However, this method will only confirm age, and it doesn't mean a piece without wear is not old.

If you will carefully pick up the piece of crackle glass you have found and feel the weight of the glass, you will find that your heavier and thicker pieces, in comparison to other pieces the same size, will be a better grade of glass and in most cases an older piece. Normally, a reproduced piece of crackle glass will be light weight and in most instances a very thin glass.

A sensitive touch can sometimes detect newer glass. A specimen of crackle that has sharp pieces of glass that prick or grab when you slide your hand across it is most likely a newer piece. Older pieces are smoother to the touch. The reproductions that are coming in from other countries usually have sharp cut edges, instead of the smooth and round finish found on most of the original pieces.

Blenko sandblasted their name on a few pieces during the 1959 and 1960 years. Sometimes a piece of crackle glass with the manufacturer's label still intact can be found. Blenko's silver foil label in the shape of an open hand with black letters that read "Blenko Handcraft" was used until the mid-1980s.

The Bischoff labels changed during their 1922-1996 years. Lancaster Colony and Sloan Glass, Inc. continued the use of the Bischoff labels during the years they operated out of the Bischoff building and continued the use of their molds (1963-1964, 1964-1996). These labels were black on silver; silver on black; silver on black with an elf; and silver on dark green with an elf.

The Hamon label also changed, with the first label being a pink on blue with the name Diana written across the label. Next came the label shaped like the state of West Virginia with the Hamon name. Then a silver with green and black was used with a glass blower and the Hamon name.

From 1949 until 1969, the Pilgrim Company's primary production was crackle glass. The Pilgrim Company changed its labels through the years. A yellow label was used in the beginning. A piece found with this color Pilgrim label would indicate an older piece; the next label was black; then white and silver; then black, blue, and white; black, red, and white; and finally black and white. These labels can be used in accurately identifying the age of a piece of Pilgrim crackle glass. The Pilgrim Company also began making their glass pitchers with clear handles rather than colored handles in the early 1960s.

The Rainbow Art Glass Company made crackle glass from 1954 until 1979. Rainbow also used different labels, the first being the shape of an open fan, or peacock feathers, black on silver, with the name Rainbow across it. The glass bubble shape was used in later years in black on silver, or red on silver. The red was used on the company's seconds.

The Dereume label was found in blue and gold, and it reads Dereume Glass Company, West Virginia Glass.

Company labels that never changed would only tell you that the piece was made during the years crackle glass was produced by that company. I am only aware of one Kanawha label used during the 1957-1987 years Kanawha produced crackle glass. It is gold with black letters spelling Kanawha.

Crackle glass has been manufactured for many, many years but was the most popular in the 1940s through the 1960s. A large percentage of crackle glass produced during those years came from West Virginia.

Without knowing the previous owner of a piece of crackle and the history behind it, it is most difficult for a freshman crackle glass collector to date a piece of crackle glass. Experience is the key...that is why I have taken the time to share my experience and knowledge with you in this book. Without the help of old company catalogs, signed, marked or labeled pieces, in-depth knowledge and experienced handling of hundreds of pieces of crackle is your best tool in determining the age of an unidentified piece of crackle glass.

Older Pieces

Older pieces of crackle glass are recognized by the experienced naked eye. Represented L-R: Unidentified, Fry, and Hamon.

25

Cranberry cruet with a round crackled stopper, my overall favorite, 1940s, H. 6.75", B. 5.5", T. 2.5". Value $100-$150.

Green #710 Hamon cruet with exquisite stopper, 1950s, H. 10", B. 6" T. 5.5". Value $100-$150.

Topaz Fry lemonade pitcher with jade green handle and finial on lid, 1901-1933, H. 11". Value $125-$175.

Triangle iridescent unidentified craquel vase. *Courtesy of Jane and Donald Thompson.* Value $25-$35.

Reproductions

Reproductions, like older pieces, can also be identified by sight and touch. L-R: Light rose from Taiwan and light blue from China. Notice the sharp cut edges of the mouths of both these pieces.

Popular blue International Silver Company candle holder, made in China. Sharp cut edge at mouth, sold in a lot of flea markets. H. 3". *Courtesy of Jane and Donald Thompson.* Value $5-$10.

Bottom of blue candle holder showing the China label.

Bottom of Lilac vase showing the Taiwan label.

Lilac Toyo vase with sharp cut edge at mouth, made in Taiwan, H. 9". *Courtesy of Lucille Holcomb.* Value $10-$15.

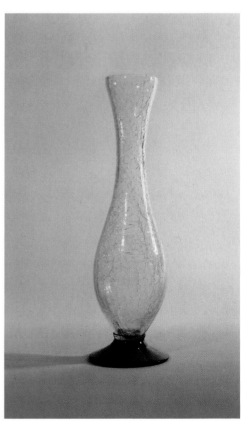

Clear unidentified vase with plastic blue foot, made in Belgium, sharp cut edge at mouth, H. 9.5". *Courtesy of Dana Noggle.* Value $10-$15.

Pricing Crackle Glass

There are those who feel twenty to thirty dollars is too much to ask for a miniature pitcher. Some say five to ten dollars is sufficient. These people have not been out beating the bushes and looking for crackle glass lately. My husband and I paid five to ten dollars for small pieces of crackle glass on a regular basis years ago. The demand for this glass with the growing number of collectors has made it much more difficult to find...much less for five dollars.

In the last year, I have not seen a piece of crackle glass for less than eighteen dollars, and that is for the very small pieces. Of course, most people realize it is hard to get book value, and most dealers price at about fifty percent of book. In my opinion, the prices in this book are reasonable and fair market value.

Crackle glass is the up and coming thing for treasure hunters. Each piece I own is a prized possession. I have shared some of my collection as gifts but only with a very few close friends and family.

My husband and I have, in the past seven years, spent as much as ninety-five dollars for a piece or crackle glass; and if I found a very unique piece today, I would realize the value and would be willing to pay much more.

To arrive at a base price for a piece of crackle glass, I take the piece and compare prices from similar pieces sold at antique auctions, antique shops, antique shows, and flea markets.

Age and quality of each piece most often have been included in the sample base prices others have established. I am extremely careful, however, that the much deserved value and respect is given to older pieces, as well as quality and superb craftsmanship in each individual specimen. Age most often gives character to a piece that is recognizable to the experienced naked eye. By looking and examining closely the lines, the shape, the extent of the wear marks on the bottom, and the unique characteristics, an approximate age and sometimes a manufacturer come to mind. Touching the smooth lines and feeling the weight and texture all go into placing a justifiable age and quality on each treasured piece. Experience in handling each piece of glass itself is by far the key tool used in judging quality and determining age for the purpose of setting its worth.

After examining a piece carefully, if I feel the piece is under priced and enough credit was not given in the base price others have set, I adjust the price accordingly. Also, if I feel too much credit is given to a newer piece or one with poor quality or craftsmanship, I make that adjustment as well.

Once I have a base price for a similar piece priced elsewhere and my adjustments are made, I go to my guide of important factors that should be considered before raising or lowering prices on crackle glass any further...my five most collectible categories. Looking at the specific characteristics of each piece I grade it according to these guidelines: 1) Colors (both most expensive to produce and rare colors); 2) Shapes (both rare and oversized); 3) Stoppered Pieces (both cruets and decanters); 4) Identified Pieces (marked, labeled, and numbered); and 5) Signed Pieces. Please see the Most Collectible Guidelines found in Chapter Two, which is my final stage used in setting prices.

If a piece that has a base price of twenty-five dollars falls into one of the first four most collectible categories, the price would be adjusted upward by twenty percent. This would raise the price by five dollars, putting the value at thirty dollars. If this same piece falls into two categories, another five dollars would be added, giving a price of thirty-five dollars to the piece, and so on.

Then, finally, I look for the most rare characteristic of all in crackle glass...signed pieces. If you have a piece with an artist's signature engraved on the bottom...your piece has at least doubled in value. Your piece is now worth seventy dollars.

This is basically how I arrive at my prices...However, at certain times, you find a piece that just intrigues you. This piece would be given a higher price just because you feel an attachment to the piece. I found a piece of cranberry crackle. The bottle was shaped like the bottle in "I Dream of Jeannie," except smaller. The little round stopper is crackled, and, to me, this piece just has unmistakable character. I have a piece of Fry crackle glass I feel the same way about. These pieces would carry a very heavy price tag simply because I really like them and don't care if I ever sell them. This is the way it is with crackle glass. The bottom line is—you can have guidelines, but the seller sets the prices; and sometimes there is no rhyme or reason for the differentiation of crackle glass prices from one dealer to the next. I give a piece of crackle glass a range, due to the fact that different areas and different dealers' prices will vary.

After adjusting the piece due to positive characteristics, I then look for the negative. Any chip or broken place (which is hard to detect in this type of glass) will lower the price. Holding the glass to the light and rolling the piece while you rub your fingers across the suspected break can help determine if there is a break or crack in the glass. If a defect is found, the value of the piece falls by at least fifty percent. Sometimes the piece is worthless, according to the extent of the damage. Please note that I do not consider bubbles, lines, bumps, or color variation in a piece of crackle as a defect. To me these blemishes only add character to a piece and do not affect its value.

Going back to our make believe piece of crackle valued at seventy dollars, let's say this piece had a tiny chip on the handle. The value is now reduced to thirty-five dollars. If the major part of the handle is missing, your piece of crackle glass can be discarded as worthless...unless, of course, it happened to belong to your great-grandmother, in which case this piece is priceless and would never be sold anyway.

A signed piece of crackle glass, if one should be so lucky to find it at a price they could afford, would be so rare that only the finders could decide if they could ever part with it and what price they would ask if they did. These type of finds are rare, but they do happen...just keep looking, because that million-dollar piece is out there; and you just might be the one to find it. Happy hunting!

2. The Five Most Collectible Categories

Most Collectible Guidelines

These Five Collectible Areas Increase the Value of Crackle Glass:

Numbers 1-4	Characteristics will increase the value of a piece of crackle glass by 20%.
Number 5	Characteristic will increase the value of a piece of crackle glass by at least 50%.

Most collectible categories represented L-R: Expensive color to produce, signed, two expensive colors to produce, two rare colors, and expensive color to produce.

Most collectible categories represented L-R: Unusual color,
unusual shape, stoppered, rare color, signed, and two stoppered.

Most collectible categories represented L-R: Unusual shape,
stoppered, labeled, and unusual shape.

1. COLORS
a. Most Expensive Colors To Produce (Due to expense of certain chemicals used in producing these colors)
  1. Ruby Red
  2. Cobalt Blue
  3. Cranberry
  4. Amberina (Shading from a dark red or orange to a light amber)
b. Most Rare and Unusual Colors (Colors hard to find)
  1. Vaseline (A light green-yellow color with a glossy Vaseline look)
  2. Pink or Cranberry
  3. Charcoal
  4. Brown
  5. Amethyst
  6. Ice Blue
  7. Two or More Colors or a Two-Tone Piece (An amberina or amberina look...going from a darker to a lighter color.)
  8. Any Rare Color

Most Expensive Colors To Produce

Colors that require expensive chemicals to make, like gold, sold for higher prices in most companies. These pieces are most sought after and demand a higher price. These colors are limited to amberina, cobalt blue, ruby red, and cranberry. Represented L-R: Rainbow, Blenko, Rainbow, and Kanawha/Hamon.

Amberina pieces represented L-R: Unidentified tea pitcher, Kanawha miniature pitcher, and Rainbow vase with applied neck decoration. This amberina color is very popular and most plentiful.

Red unidentified ashtray, 1950-1960. Value $25-$35.

Cobalt blue Blenko basket, this color is very rare. 1950-1955, H. 7.5". Value $100-$150.

Rare and Unusual Colors

Rare and Unusual Colors are difficult to find. Represented L-R: two-tone (dark yellow fading to a very light yellow), brown, light baby blue, deep rose or cranberry, and light amethyst.

Amberina #6424 Blenko candle holder, 1946-1966, H. 5.5". Value $30-$40.

Light blue iridescent unidentified vase. H. 8". *Courtesy of Jane and Donald Thompson.* Value $40-$50.

Dark brown Pilgrim jug, 1949-1959, H. 6". *Courtesy of Jane and Donald Thompson.* Value $30-$40.

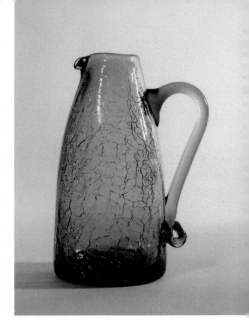

Light amethyst Pilgrim miniature pitcher, marked, 1949-1959, H. 4". Value $25-$35.

Yellow fading to a lighter yellow Pilgrim pinched vase, marked, 1949-1969, H. 5". *Courtesy of Jane and Donald Thompson.* Value $25-$35.

Baby blue Pilgrim miniature vase, 1949-1969, 5". *Courtesy of Jane and Donald Thompson.* Value $20-$25.

Dark brown Pilgrim miniature pitcher, 1949-1959, H. 4". Value $20-$25.

Emerald green Pilgrim miniature pitcher, 1960-1969, H. 4.5". Value $20-$25.

Cranberry unidentified cruet with iridescent look and a round crackled stopper, very old (was marked Czechoslovakia by the seller), a very rare color, H. 6.75", B. 5.5", T. 2.5". Value $100-$150.

Black amethyst Pilgrim miniature pitcher, 1960-1969, very rare color, H. 4.5". *Courtesy of Dana Noggle.* Value $30-$40.

Peach Rainbow Cruet, 1954-1973, H. 6", B. 5", T. 2.25". *Courtesy of Jane and Donald Thompson.* Value $50-$75.

Dark turquoise Kanawha cylinder, 1959-1987, H. 14". Value $25-$35.

Light brown Pilgrim vase with clear rope neck, 1949-1969, H. 4.25". *Courtesy of Jane and Donald Thompson.* Value $25-$35.

Orange Rainbow cruet, 1954-1973, H. 6.5", B. 5", T. 2.5". *Courtesy of Jane and Donald Thompson.* Value $50-$75.

Brown fluted mouth unidentified vase, possibly made by Smith's Old-Timer, Hand blown Glass, Fort Smith, Arkansas. H. 9.5". *Courtesy of Jane and Donald Thompson.* Value $40-$50.

Dark amethyst Rainbow pitcher, very rare color, 1954-1973, H. 5". *Courtesy of Dana Noggle.* Value $35-$45.

35

Pale blue fluted mouth unidentified vase, possibly made by Smith's Old-Timer, Hand blown Glass, Fort Smith, Arkansas. H. 9". *Courtesy of Jane and Donald Thompson.* Value $50-$75.

Rare and Unusual Shapes

Rare and unusual shapes represented L-R: Rainbow, Blenko, Kanawha, and Rainbow.

Gray Pilgrim candy dish, 1949-1969, 3 x 4.5". Value $25-$35.

2. SHAPES & STYLES
   a. Most Rare and Unusual Shapes (Shapes difficult to find)
      1. Fruit
      2. Ink Well
      3. Mantel Candle Holders
      4. Any Very Unusually Shaped Piece
   b. Oversized Pieces (Very rare)
      1. Lamps
      2. Giant Bottles
      3. Decanters
      4. Any Oversized Piece

Black wrought iron mantle candle holders with cranberry painted Rainbow globes, 1950-1963, globe H. 4". *Courtesy of Pat Paschall.* Value $75-$100 (pair).

Rare and unusual shapes represented L-R: three unidentified and Pilgrim.

Green #5 Pilgrim swan candy dish (crackled only on the bottom), 1949-1969, H. 5.5". Value $50-$75.

Amberina #6424 Blenko candle holders, 1950-1960, H. 5.5". Value $60-$80 (pair).

Ruby red Hamon apple, 1950-1770, H. 4". *Courtesy of Brenda Manning.* Value $40-$50.

Ruby red Kanawha apple, 1959-1987, H. 3.25". *Courtesy of Pat Paschall.* Value $40-$50.

Green #6424 Blenko candle holder, 1950-1960, H. 6". Value $25-$35.

Amber #503 Rainbow top hat vase, 1954-1973, H. 2.5". Value $25-$35.

Blue vase with tie around the neck, probably Blenko, 1940-1960, H. 6.5". *Courtesy of Jane and Donald Thompson.* Value $40-$50.

Amberina unidentified wine glasses, rare, H. 4.75". Value $50-$75 (pair).

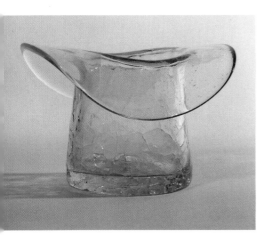

Light blue #M-14 Pilgrim top hat vase, 1949-1969, H. 2.5". *Courtesy of Jane and Donald Thompson.* Value $30-$40.

Clear unidentified jelly jar with bronze top and glass spoon, H. 5". *Courtesy of Jane and Donald Thompson.* Value $30-$40.

Amber Pilgrim cream and sugar, 1949-1959, H. 3". Value $50-$75 (set).

Light green vase, probably Bischoff, 1922-1963, H. 8.5". *Courtesy of Jane and Donald Thompson.* Value $50-$75.

Green unidentified ink well, H. 2". Value $15-$20.

Two-tone yellow Blenko vase with applied ruby red rope, 1946-1986, H. 8". Value $50-$75.

Oversized Items

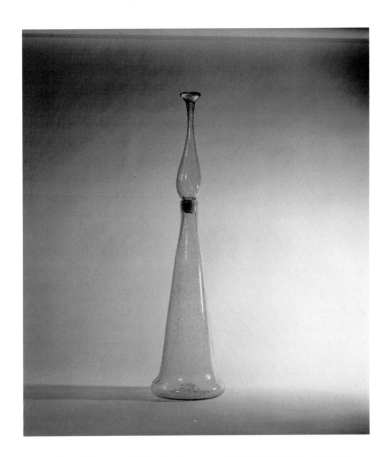

Oversize Blenko art with a Kanawha apple to compare the size.

Bright yellow #6029 Blenko decanter, 1963, H. 25.5", B. 17", T. 10.25". *Courtesy of Dana Noggle.* Value $75-$100.

Crystal unidentified crackle glass lamp, 1950-1970, H. 35". Value $50-$75.

Green #6123 Blenko bottle, 1963, H. 25". Value $50-$75.

Stoppered pieces represented L-R: Blenko, Pilgrim, Rainbow,
Unidentified, Rainbow, and Hamon.

Stoppered pieces represented L-R: Pilgrim, Rainbow, Blenko,
Rainbow, and Blenko.

3. STOPPERED PIECES Cruets (a small bottle with a stopper) and Decanters with the Original Stopper (Stoppered pieces take more time and talent to create. Also, it is hard to find a piece with its original stopper, as through the years they were most often lost or broken)

Finding an item with the inside of the mouth ground indicates the piece had a stopper at one time. A piece without the original stopper would lower its value. Represented is a green Pilgrim cruet without the stopper.

Three Rainbow brilliant colored cruets. These were left to my husband by his mom and were the beginning of our love for crackle glass.

Decanters and cruets are very collectible and usually carry a very heavy price tag because two separate items in one (stopper and bottle) makes it even more difficult to survive through the years without breakage. Represented L-R: clear unidentified decanter, green Hamon decanter, and amberina Rainbow cruet.

Amberina Blenko decanter, H. 13", B. 10.75, T. 3.5". Value $50-$75.

Blue Blenko decanter, H. 11.5", B. 7", T. 5.5". *Courtesy of Jane and Donald Thompson.* Value $40-$50.

Olive green Blenko decanter, H. 15", B. 11.5", T. 4". *Courtesy of Jane and Donald Thompson.* Value $40-$50.

Olive green Blenko decanter with an unusual stopper the shape of a tiny bottle, 1963, H. 14.5", B. 10", T. 4.25". *Courtesy of Jane and Donald Thompson.* Value $50-$75.

Topaz #627 Blenko decanter, 1962, H. 12", B. 10", T. 3.5". *Courtesy of Jane and Donald Thompson.* Value $40-$50.

Clear #49 Blenko decanter with cobalt blue stopper, 1940-1960, H. 11", B. 9.25", T. 3". *Courtesy of Jane and Donald Thompson.* Value $45-$55.

Sea green and yellow #37 Blenko decanters, 1962, H. 12.5", B. 9",
T. 5". *Courtesy of Jane and Donald Thompson*, $50-$75 (each).

Amethyst #37 Blenko decanter (stopper is broken), 1960, H.
12.5", B.10", T. 4.5". Value $50-$75

Amberina #920 Blenko oversized decanter designed by Winslow
Anderson, H. 22.25", B. 16.5", T. 7.5". *Courtesy of Jane and
Donald Thompson.* Value $75-$100.

Orange amberina #920 Blenko decanter designed by Winslow
Anderson, H. 16.5", B. 11.75", T. 6.25". *Courtesy of Jane and
Donald Thompson.* Value $55-$80.

Light olive green #920 Blenko decanter designed by Winslow
Anderson, H. 16.5", B. 12", T. 5.5". *Courtesy of Dana Noggle.*
Value $45-$55.

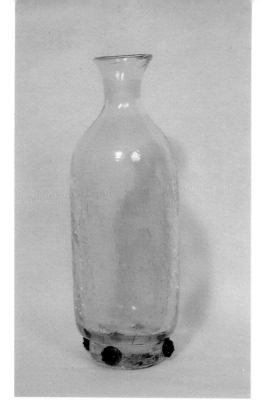

Clear #445 Blenko decanter with applied amethyst rosettes, missing the stopper (stopper should be the color of the rosettes), 1940-1950, H. 10.5". *Courtesy of Jane and Donald Thompson.* Value $30-$40.

Green #710 Hamon cruet with beautiful stopper, 1950s, H. 10", B. 6", T. 5.5". Value $100-$150.

Green #C112 Pilgrim cruet, 1959-1969, H. 6", B. 4.5", T. 2.5". *Courtesy of Dana Noggle.* Value $40-$50.

Large amberina #6211 Blenko decanter...missing the stopper, 1962, H. 12". Value $35-$45.

Tangerine #C112 Pilgrim cruet, 1959-1969, H. 6", B. 4.5", T. 2.5". Value $50-$75.

Ruby red #23 Pilgrim decanter, 1959-1969, H. 18.5", B. 12", T. 7.5". Value $50-$75.

44

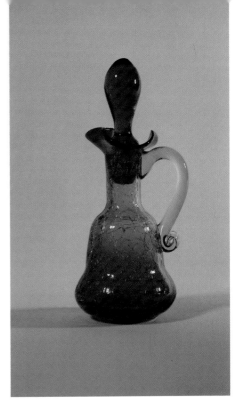

Yellow #20 Pilgrim decanter...missing the stopper, 1949-1969, H. 9". *Courtesy of Jane and Donald Thompson.* Value $30-$40.

Turquoise #402 Rainbow cruet, 1954-1973, H. 6.5", B. 4.5", T. 3.5". Value $50-$75.

Orange Amberina #401 Rainbow cruet, 1954-1973, H. 7", B. 6", T. 2". Value $50-$75.

Clear unidentified decanter, H. 9.5", B. 7", T. 3". Value $40-$50.

Red Rainbow cruet, 1954-1973, H. 8", B. 6", T. 3". Value $50-$75.

Amber #687 Rainbow cruet, 1954-1973, H. 7", B. 6", T. 2". Value $45-$55.

Ruby red Pilgrim cruet, 1949-1969, H. 6.25", B. 5.25", T. 2.25". *Courtesy of Pat Paschall.* Value $50-$75.

Emerald green #330 Rainbow decanter with exquisite stopper, 1954-1973, H. 13.5", B. 6", T. 9.5" (Note: the stopper is longer than the decanter). Value $100-$150.

Amberina Rainbow decanter (it could be a vase as the mouth is not ground), 1954-1973, H. 10", B. 7.75", T. 4". Value $50-$75.

Two ruby red Rainbow decanters, (not the original stoppers), 1954-1973, H. L-R: 11" and 14". Value $75-$100 (set).

4. IDENTIFIED PIECES

a. Marked (Any mark that will identify the manufacturing company. Blenko and Pilgrim pieces are the only marked pieces of crackle glass I have found.)

　1. Blenko **sandblasted** their name on the bottom of their pieces in 1959 and 1960.

　2. Pilgrim **Measle Mark** (This mark looks like tiny dots and is made by a file touching the bottom of the piece before it is completely dry. It is also known as the Strawberry Mark.)

　3. Pilgrim **Water Waves** (This mark looks like wavy lines and is made by the end of the file touching the bottom of the piece before it is completely dry.)

b. Labeled (A paper label showing the original manufacturer's name still on the piece of crackle glass)

c. Numbered (Some of the Kanawha molds have numbers that show on the bottom of the glass.)

Identified crackle glass represented L-R: Two marked Pilgrim,
labeled Rainbow, numbered Kanawha, and marked Pilgrim.

Identified pieces represented L-R: Two signed pieces and two
marked pieces.

Light blue #389 Blenko seed vase, 1946-1953, H. 7". *Courtesy of Dana Noggle.* Value $75-$100.

Dark green Bischoff vase, 1922-1963, H. 4". Value $25-$35.

Orange/yellow Heritage miniature pitcher, H. 4.25". *Courtesy of Jane and Donald Thompson.* Value $25-$35.

Pieces of crackle glass with manufacturers labels are rare. Represented L-R: Blenko, Pilgrim, Blenko, Rainbow, and Pilgrim.

Pink Iridescent #7576 P8 Fenton basket with label, 1992-1993, H. 11". Value $100-$150.

Fenton basket with our newest addition to our family inside. The value just went up.

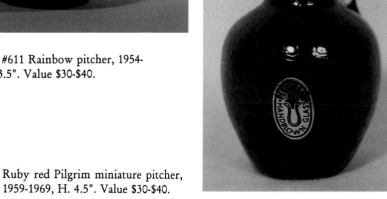

Ruby red #611 Rainbow pitcher, 1954-1973, H. 3.5". Value $30-$40.

Emerald green Blenko vase, 1950-1960, H. 9.5". *Courtesy of Dana Noggle.* Value $50-$75.

Ruby red Pilgrim miniature pitcher, 1959-1969, H. 4.5". Value $30-$40.

Two dark green #755 Pilgrim jugs, 1949-1959, H. 4". *Courtesy of Kelly Brown.* Value $40-$50 (pair).

Ruby red #R202 Rainbow pitcher, 1954-1973, H. 4.5". *Courtesy of Danielle Howle.* Value $40-$50.

Amber #343 Rainbow decanter (Note: red Rainbow labels identified their seconds. These pieces were sent to the Rainbow retail store.), 1954-1973, H. 8". *Courtesy of Jane and Donald Thompson.* Value $50-$75.

Ruby red Rainbow vase. (Note: the early Rainbow label), 1950s, H. 4.5". Value $40-$50.

Amberina #15 Kanawha mold miniature pitcher (label reads "Souvenir of Williamsburg, Virginia"), 1959-1987, H. 5.5". Value $30-$40.

Amberina #17 Kanawha vase, 1959-1987, H. 5.5". Value $30-$40.

Amberina #636 Blenko decanter, 1963, H. 8", B. 6", T. 3.75". Value $50-$75.

Bottom of the Cranberry Williamsburg piece showing the manufacturer's label. Without a label this piece would probably be identified as a Kanawha piece because Williamsburg used Kanawha molds.

Cranberry assortment #8 Williamsburg miniature pitcher. Very few pieces of crackle glass were made by Williamsburg, very rare color, 1971-mid-1970s, H. 8.25". Value $50-$75.

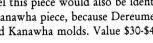

Ruby red #1138 Kanawha pitcher, made by Hamon, 1969-1980. *Courtesy of Pat Paschall.* Value $50-$75.

Blue #6-8 Dereume bud vase. Without a label this piece would also be identified as a Kanawha piece, because Dereume also used Kanawha molds. Value $30-$40.

Red Blenko Bowl with a sandblasted mark that reads "© Blenko" on the bottom. Blenko did this in 1959 and 1960 in an attempt to patent their shapes. 4 x 6.5". Value $75-$100.

Red #73 Pilgrim vase with rope neck. This piece has a Pilgrim "measle mark" on the bottom, as seen in the following illustration. H. 11". *Courtesy of Jane and Donald Thompson.* Value $70-$95.

Light amethyst and ruby red Pilgrim miniature pitchers. The one on the left has a Pilgrim "water wave" mark on the bottom, as seen in the following illustration.

Bottom of Red #73 Pilgrim vase with rope neck showing the tiny dots on the bottom of the piece. This "measle mark" was made when Pilgrim glass blowers touched the bottom of the piece with a file.

Bottom of light amethyst miniature pitcher showing the broken wave lines on the bottom of this piece. This "water wave" mark was made when Pilgrim glass blowers touched the bottom of the piece with a file.

Numbered Pieces

This yellow #14 Kanawha piece has the number 14 made into the mold and shows on the bottom. This is the first piece I've ever seen numbered. Number 14 is the catalog number as well as the mold number. 1959-1987, H. 5". *Courtesy of Jane and Donald Thompson.* Value $40-$50.

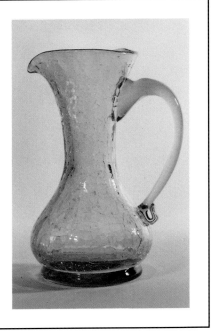

This Vaseline Pilgrim cup is signed by the glass blower with his initials on the bottom. Vaseline glass turns a bright yellow color under ultra violet rays. 1949-1959, H. 8". *Courtesy of Dana Noggle.* Value $50-$75.

5. SIGNED (A piece of crackle glass with the signature of the artist engraved on the bottom of the specimen)

Two signed pieces.

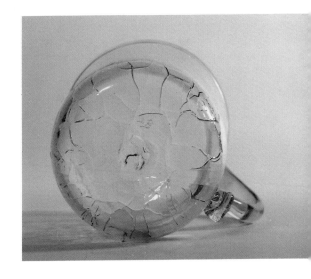

The D. B. initials on the bottom of this piece identifies the maker. Either Dale Burd or Doug Brewer (both Pilgrim glass blowers) most likely gave birth to this piece of art work.

This cobalt blue mug has a custom sized handle made especially for Dana Noggle. Dana witnessed this mug being blown at the Georgia Renaissance Festival in Fairburn, Georgia, in 1990 by R. Foster. H. 6.5". Value $40-$50.

Bottom of Dana Noggle's cobalt blue mug showing the signature of the artist and the year of creation, R. Foster '90.

53

3. Identification of Crackle Glass Manufacturers, 1853-1940

Crackle Glass Manufacturers 1853-1930

Federal Glass Company

The Federal Glass Company out of Columbus, Ohio, started making crackled glass by hand in 1900. In the 1920s, automation took over, and in 1930 this company began making glass pieces in colors.

In the 1928 Federal Glass Catalog, three sets of crackle glass were shown: Jack Frost Water Set, Iced Tea Set, and Lemonade Set. These sets were all in crystal, and had a covered pitcher and six glasses making up the set. The styles of each were slightly different.

D.C. Jenkins Company

D.C. Jenkins became the president of the Kokomo Glass Company in Kokomo, Indiana, in 1901. In 1913 a second plant was opened in Arcadia, Indiana. The business was eventually named after Mr. Jenkins (D.C. Jenkins Glass Company) and was in operation until his death in 1932.

The Jenkins catalogs dating 1927-1931 show two styles of a one-half gallon covered tea pitcher in crackle. They made these lines in green and crystal only.

Macbeth-Evans Glass Company

The Macbeth-Evans Glass Company was established in 1899. This company consisted of two already renowned glass firms: Macbeth and Evans. With a just-patented glass blowing machine and their combined reputations, these companies joined to make a new name several times prominent in glass history. Many of our most desired colors today were possible due to Macbeth's new venture into machine-made colored glass. In 1937, the firm was bought by Corning Glass Works of Corning, New York. In the 1940s, jugs and tumblers were very big, and they continued to be produced under the MacBeth-Evans name.

Pages from a 1931 catalog show two emerald green water crackled iced tea sets marked "Scrabble" (pattern name). The pitchers were the same, but the glasses were shaped differently. Also shown were other styles of glasses, all in the emerald green color. A pattern for a crackled glass jug designed by E. R. Worcester and filed on June 8, 1927, was shown in this catalog as well. This jug was purchased by the MacBeth-Evans Glass Company in emerald green and crystal in 1928. The pattern name for this piece was "Spindle Jug."

McKee Glass Company

McKee and Brothers began their company in 1853. In 1903, after many name changes, the firm was reorganized and named the McKee Glass Company. That name was used until 1951, when the company was sold to Thatcher Glass Company. The McKee Division of the Thatcher Glass Company was then used.

In a 1924 ad, McKee advertised innovation crackled glassware for spring and summer. They showed an iced tea set with covered pitcher and six glasses (the crackles appear larger and thicker than regular crackle glass). This new line was advertised as being made in crystal, blue, amber, canary, green, and amethyst. They also stated "a colored handle could be furnished if so desired." A list of their new line of crackle glass was given as follows: iced tea set (shown), water sets (uncovered), grape juice sets, beverage sets, console sets, salad plates, handled lunch plates, and cheese and cracker sets which could be purchased in any of the colors listed previously.

U.S. Glass Company

The U.S. Glass Company was established in 1891. The merger was a combined effort of eighteen glass companies to join forces in an effort to survive. Over the years, some of the factories were lost due to various reasons. In 1938, the main office moved from Pittsburgh to Tiffin. At that time only the new office and the Pittsburgh office were left. By 1951, only Tiffin had survived.

In an old 1924 catalog, the U.S. Glass Company advertised "Stripple" (the pattern of six glasses shown) in green. It also stated that the jug shown (which looks like a tea pitcher) also came cracquelled (notice spelling) in blue and canary. The catalog also featured a different style water pitcher set with a covered pitcher and six glasses. It was labeled Craquel (a different spelling of crackle): crystal with green trim.

Bartlett-Collins
Sapulpa, Oklahoma Glass House

In 1914, an Oklahoma man named Bartlett and an East Coast man named Collins teamed up and founded the Sapulpa, Oklahoma Glass House. This company was known especially for its tableware. The company was hand operated until 1941, at which time the machines took over.

In an old catalog, a crackled jug (which looks like a pitcher) was shown with six 13 ounce tumblers. The ad indicated that in 1927 this company produced rose, amber, and crystal iridescent colors.

George Borgfeldt and Company

In a 1926 ad, Geo. Borgfeldt & Company out of New York premiered a water set in green mould crackled glass with a 9" jug (water pitcher) and six 4.75" glasses. "Embodying the usually high-priced cone shaped footed jug and tumblers for the first time at a popular price. May be retailed at $1.19 or lower if you choose," the ad read.

H.C. Fry Glass Company

The H.C. Fry Glass Company out of Rochester, Pennsylvania, was in business from 1901 until 1933 when the company was sold to the Libby Company. They manufactured what they referred to as a lemonade set, a covered pitcher and six tumblers. The handle and finial on the lid were jade green or delft blue for most of their accessories.

Summary—1853-1930s

(This information was compiled using information found in *Colored Glassware Of The Depression Era 2*, by Hazel Marie Weatherman, with the exception of the Fry Glass Company where *The Collector's Encyclopedia Of Fry Glass*, by the H.C. Fry Glass Society was used.)

Companies that produced crackle glass in the earlier years, 1853-1930s, were located throughout the United States. These companies had a lot of similarities:

1) They all produced crackle glass by hand until around the 1920s.
2) They only produced crystal pieces until the 1920-1930s when a couple of other colors began being produced...with green being the primary "other" color. (McKee did list a little wider variety of colors.)
3) They all produced pitchers (covered and uncovered), different styles of glasses, pitcher sets (with pitcher and six glasses)...and little else. (McKee did list plates with cheese and cracker sets.)
4) All pieces manufactured during this era were "useful" items. No items were manufactured for the sole purpose of decoration or beauty.
5) Identification of styles mentioned about each company (with the exception of H.C. Fry Company) can be identified in *Colored Glassware Of The Depression Era 2* by Hazel Marie Weatherman.
6) The H.C. Fry Company crackle glass pieces can be identified in *The Collector's Encyclopedia Of Fry Glass*, by the Fry Glass Society, 1901-1933.

Crackle Glass Manufacturers
1930-1940
(These Companies Produced Only
a Small Quantity of Crackle Glass)

Bonita Glass Company
Huntington, West Virginia

Bonita Glass Company advertising in the April 1946 Giftware showed a new Robert P. Pierce line done in crackle glass. There were fourteen items in this ad: a swan dish, trumpet vase, three top hat vases, four fluted vases, one pinched vase, two plain vases, and two different sizes of glasses. In its time Bonita may have been a major producer of crackle glass.

The Bruce and Emch Glass Company
Huntington, West Virginia

This company was in business during the 1940s. An old company receipt tablet page, sent to me by Dean Six, reads: The Bruce and Emch Glass Company, Artistic Hand Made—Crystal, Crackled and Colors, 523 Jackson Avenue, Huntington, West Virginia, 194_, C. Emch, phone 22933, and J.R. Bruce, phone 28134.

Heritage Glass Company

Little is known about Heritage. Although I was told they operated out of Salem, West Virginia, I have been unable to verify that information.

I have photographed one piece of Heritage art. This piece still carried the label that read Heritage. Although the label is very worn and the city could not be detected, we could make out the state of West Virginia. The piece is a small orange miniature pitcher.

The Imperial Glass Corporation
Bellaire, Ohio

Although Imperial was established in 1901, Candlewick took the line in the mid-1930s and was produced until 1982 when the company went bankrupt. Imperial produced only a few experimental pieces of crackle glass in their candlewick line.

In 1940 Imperial acquired Central Glassworks of Wheeling, West Virginia. In 1958 Imperial purchased the molds of A.H. Heisey and Company, and in 1960 Cambridge Glass Company of Cambridge, Ohio, was purchased. In 1973 Imperial became a subsidiary of Lenox, Incorporated.

Moncer Glass Company
Huntington, West Virginia

A Moncer Glass pamphlet that is not dated tells of a Sword Fish that can be purchased in blue, green, amber, and crystal. This piece could be purchased in decorated or crackled glass. In this same pamphlet, a pinched, pint decanter was advertised in blue violet, emerald green, gold amber, and crystal. These decanters were offered in crackle as well as decorated colored glass.

Spring Valley Glass Company
Huntington, West Virginia

Spring Valley Glass Company of Huntington, West Virginia, which operated from 1942 until after 1948, made a crackle glass pinched decanter with an unusual shaped stopper. This piece, manufactured in 1942 and listed in the Budget Glass Factory Directory for 1945, used a tiny pinched vase for the stopper. It was produced in clear or clear with cranberry trim. Pilgrim Glass Factory also carried a piece similar to this one.

Voglesong Glass Company

I was told Voglesong operated out of Huntington, West Virginia, 1949 through 1951, but this information has not been confirmed. They most often produce twisted trumpet interlocking flower vases.

West Virginia Glass Specialty Company
Weston, West Virginia

West Virginia Glass Specialty Company premiered a new line of crackle glass in four different fluted mouth vases in an ad in the *Crockery and Glass Journal* for December, 1949. This new line was called Marine Ripple. West Virginia Glass Specialty Company operated out of Weston, West Virginia, and produced crackle glass for only a short period of time.

4. 1930-1990s Major Producer's History and their "Most Plentiful" Art Illustrations

Most Plentiful Shapes and Colors

The three most plentiful shapes are vases, pitchers, and jugs. Companies represented L-R: Blenko, Pilgrim, Dereume, Fry, three Pilgrim, and Bischoff.

Pitchers, jugs, and vases are the three most plentiful shapes to find. Represented L-R: Pilgrim, Blenko, and Rainbow.

Although miniature pitchers are the most plentiful, all size pitchers are very common. Represented L-R: Rainbow, Pilgrim, Fry, and two Pilgrim.

Pitchers represented; two unknown tea pitchers and four Pilgrim.

Pitchers represented L-R: Kanawha and two Rainbow.

Pitchers represented L-R: two Hamon, Pilgrim, and Rainbow.

Pitchers represented L-R: Rainbow and two Kanawha.

Vases are also plentiful. Represented L-R: Blenko, Pilgrim, and Blenko.

Vases can be found in a wide variety of colors. Represented L-R: Bischoff, unidentified, and Rainbow.

Vases come in all shapes and sizes and are very plentiful. Companies represented L-R: Dereume, Pilgrim, Blenko, Rainbow, unidentified, and Kanawha.

Yellow and amber colors are very common. Represented L-R: Blenko and three Pilgrim.

Greens, amberinas, reds, and blues are all common colors. Represented L-R: Blenko, Rainbow, Pilgrim, and Rainbow.

Jugs are also a most plentiful shape and are found most often in green, red, amberina, or amber. Companies represented L-R: Hamon, Pilgrim, Hamon, and two Pilgrim.

Bischoff Glass Company

Huntington, West Virginia
Hurricane, West Virginia
Culloden, West Virginia

Lancaster Colony

(Columbus, Ohio Division)
Culloden, West Virginia

Sloan Glass, Inc.

Culloden, West Virginia

The Bischoff Glass Company was founded in 1922 by three Bischoff brothers. They started in Huntington, West Virginia on Jackson Avenue. Between the time it opened and 1936, the business moved to Hurricane, West Virginia. In 1936, the company once again relocated, this time to Culloden, West Virginia.

It has been said that Bischoff was a master of reproductions, which appears was a common practice in the glass industry. Bischoff, however, had many wonderful and creative originals of their own, as did the other West Virginia crackle glass producers. Bischoff has many unusually shaped items, some of which take on a European look. Bischoff pieces appear to be thicker and heavier when compared to other manufacturer's pieces of the

same size. You will also find many small window sill pieces in the green and amber colors.

The Columbus, Ohio, division of Lancaster Colony, established in 1961 under the leadership of John B. Gerlach, bought the Bischoff Glass Company in 1963. One source reports that Lois Bischoff, the widow of one of the Bischoff brothers, decided to sell the company due to union problems. When Lancaster Colony purchased the business they continued operations under the Bischoff name. They continued production out of the same building using the molds of the Bischoff Glass Company.

In April of 1964, Charles P. Sloan purchased the company and continued production of glass using the styles and techniques used by Bischoff Glass Company but under the new name of Sloan Glass, Inc. Although the building carried the Sloan Glass, Inc. name, the pieces that were produced there were created by the use of Bischoff molds. Therefore, Mr. Sloan used the Bischoff labels on his pieces of artwork.

The Sloan Company's major production is lighting balls. These items are also done in crackle. Crackle glass was made until January of 1996, when ongoing legal disputes caused the operations to cease. After the problems are resolved, Mr. Sloan plans to once again put the business in operation.

Bischoff pieces have brilliant colors and unique shapes.

Blue #807 Bischoff pitcher, missing a stopper, 1922-1963, H. 11.5". *Courtesy of Jane and Donald Thompson.* Value $40-$50.

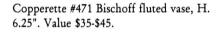

Brown #905 Bischoff vase, H. 9". *Courtesy of Dana Noggle.* Value $35-$45.

Copperette #471 Bischoff fluted vase, H. 6.25". Value $35-$45.

Green Bischoff crimped and footed vase, 1922-1963, H. 8". Value $40-$50.

Lime green Bischoff vase, 1922-1963, H. 4.5". *Courtesy of Jane and Donald Thompson.* Value $20-$30.

Eureka Glass Company
Milton, West Virginia

Blenko Glass Company
Milton, West Virginia

Blenko is one of the most popular names in the glass industry today. Although William J. Blenko, a British glass maker, had a very rough uphill climb with many setbacks, he emerged victorious in his struggle to achieve success in the glass industry.

This British glass maker who shipped stained glass to American studios moved to America in 1893 to start a glass making business in Kokomo, Indiana...only to fail and be forced to return to England in 1904. During the next ten years, he made two more attempts to set up shop in the United States. Using British glass workers in Point Marion, Pennsylvania, in 1909 and Clarksburg, West Virginia, in 1913, Blenko once again failed in his efforts and returned to London.

With persistence and determination, William J. Blenko once again brought his business to America in 1922. This time he settled in Milton, West Virginia, where he founded the Eureka Glass Company. The following year, his son, William H. Blenko, joined him. Together, they began building an empire in the glass industry.

William J. Blenko died in 1934, but not before realizing the Eureka name he had chosen for his company meant just that..."I have found it!" This time the company was on the right track and headed for a huge success. In 1933, a year before Blenko died, the name of the company was changed to the Blenko Glass Company, in honor of its founding father.

His son, William H. Blenko, brought with him new ideas. These ideas, fused with the 1000 year old tradition his father had insisted on preserving, were the combination that turned the right key and opened the doors to a long, bright, and very successful life for the Blenko Glass Company.

In 1946 William H. Blenko, Jr. joined the Blenko team, and at his father's death in 1969, took over the business and continued the traditional operations of his forefathers. In 1976, Henry Blenko, Jr.'s son Richard Deakin Blenko joined forces with his father and became active in the family business. Henry Blenko and his son Deakin run the business today.

Four generations of Blenko families have poured their lives and energies into this glass business to achieve great fame through their decorative glassware. No one deserves more credit in the success of this company than does Deakin's great-grandfather, who first had to suffer the losses before winning the race.

John Blenko's driving force was his desire to make and market hand blown stained glass in the United States. Although this is not the most successful item in the Blenko line, it is very popular and most sought after. I was told by the Blenko office that over 3000 colors have been used in the stained glass shops at Blenko. Stained glass that carries the name of Blenko today is noted for its vibrant colors, beauty, and exquisite craftsmanship.

In all the Blenko lines, superb craftsmanship and vibrant colors are a trademark. Blenko made crackle glass in many of these radiant colors and styles through the years. Most of the larger pieces of crackle glass belong to Blenko. Crackle glass first appeared in the Blenko catalogs in 1946. Although crackle glass was produced in more abundance during the 1940 through 1970 years, it is still being produced today.

Quoting from printed information mailed to me by Blenko: "The factory attracts thousands of visitors every year from all over the United States, as well as foreign countries. Here they can watch the molten glass take its final form, as Blenko craftsmen practice their skilled art. The visitor's center features a designer's corner of nine leading stained glass windows and the Blenko Museum of Historic Glass. (You will find some Blenko crackle glass displayed here.) Also there is a 'Garden of Glass' surrounding a 3 acre lake for visitors to enjoy."

Blenko's craftsmanship is exquisite, as shown here.

Blenko's craftsmanship and brilliant
colors are breath-taking.

A display of Blenko's superb art.

Blenko's spectacular hand blown glass.

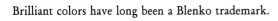

Brilliant colors have long been a Blenko trademark.

Blenko is known for their gorgeous oversized pieces of hand blown glass art.

Blenko colors are superb with a variety of over 3,000 colors, with only three of those colors shown in these #366 Blenko vases.

Clear crystal rimed and flared #482 Blenko vase with rose trim, 1940s, H. 14". Value $125-$175.

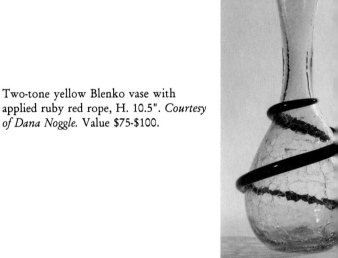

Two-tone yellow Blenko vase with applied ruby red rope, H. 10.5". *Courtesy of Dana Noggle.* Value $75-$100.

Blenko decorative craftsmanship is displayed with these beautiful vases with applied rope of a different color.

Clear flared #482 Blenko vase with applied decoration in blue, 1940s, H. 12". *Courtesy of Candace Alford Reid.* Value $125-$175.

Blue Blenko vase with applied emerald rope, H. 9.5". *Courtesy of Jane and Donald Thompson.* Value $60-$85.

Ruby red #496 Blenko vase, 1950s, H. 11.5". Value $45-$55.

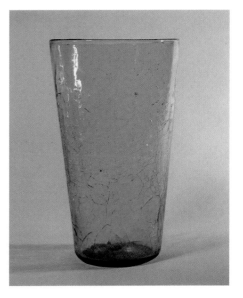

Light green #366 Blenko vase, 1950s, H. 10". Value $30-$40.

Chartreuse #390 Blenko crimped vase designed by Winslow Anderson, 1950s, H. 8". *Courtesy of Dana Noggle.* Value $85-$110.

Two-tone bright yellow to light yellow #366 Blenko vase, 1950s, H. 10". Value $30-$40.

Olive green Blenko vase, 1950s, H. 5". *Courtesy of Dana Noggle.* Value $20-$30.

Green #947 Blenko pinched vase, 1950s, H. 4". Value $15-$20.

Blue #415 Blenko pinched vase, H. 5". *Courtesy of Jane and Donald Thompson.* Value $20-$30.

Olive green #39 Blenko pinched vase, H. 5". *Courtesy of Jane and Donald Thompson.* Value $15-$20.

Olive green #415 Blenko pinched vase, 4". *Courtesy of Jane and Donald Thompson.* Value $15-$20.

Small green Blenko vase, 1950s, H. 4.5". *Courtesy of Jane and Donald Thompson.* Value $15-$20.

Small amber Blenko vase, H. 3.75". *Courtesy of Jane and Donald Thompson.* Value $15-$20.

Small olive green Blenko vase, 1950s, H. 5.75". Value $15-$20.

Red Blenko or Bischoff 411 dimpled vase, 1940-1950s, H. 6". *Courtesy of Danielle Howle.* Value $25-$35.

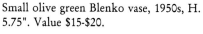

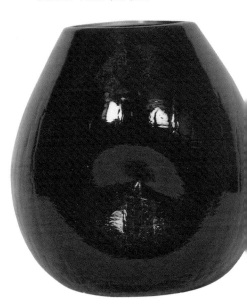

Blue Blenko pinched vase, H. 4". Value $15-$20.

Fenton Art Glass Company

Martins Ferry, Ohio
Williamstown, West Virginia

Fenton, a name that makes most glass lovers stand at attention, is a household name recognized and highly respected. In 1903, Fenton Art Glass Company was founded by two brothers, John and Frank L. Fenton, in Martins Ferry, Ohio.

When this company first began operations, the Fenton brothers were decorators of glass. They bought glass from suppliers and applied their own designs. Suppliers concerned about the competition cut their shipment of glass to the Fenton brothers. Management decided that producing their own glass was the only answer, and plans were underway to find a plant site.

Fenton catalog page showing the crackle glass Fenton produced in Green, Blue, and Pink Iridescent colors in 1993. Fenton only produced crackle glass in 1992 and 1993.

Pink Iridescent #7576 P8 Fenton basket with label, 1992-1993, H. 11". Value $100-$150.

An affordable plant site was found and purchased by John Fenton in Williamstown, West Virginia; and ground was broken for the new plant in October of 1906. By January of 1907, Fenton Art Glass was in operation. At first, times were hard; and for a few years the Fenton industry struggled.

A mysterious man showed up at the Fenton plant by way of a railroad boxcar. He came to show the Fenton brothers how to make a "new-found" glass. This new glass with rainbow colors was an iridescent glass, later known as carnival glass. This man is still nameless and in time moved on. Fenton began to prosper after the discovery of this new glass.

After piloting the Fenton ship for forty-three years, Frank L. Fenton died at the age of sixty-eight. Two other brothers, Robert and James, who were also top executive management died within the next year. Frank's oldest son, Frank M. Fenton, was assigned to the president's position, and his other son, Wilmer C. (Bill) Fenton, became the vice-president.

Both sons were very involved with their father's business for many years and carried on with their father's formula for success. Improvements were made in modern technology and administration only when these changes accented the old way. The modern operation one sees today in Williamstown is a tribute to the success of the Fenton formula.

Along with carnival glass, Fenton is also famous for its chocolate glass, cut glass, and hobnail, to name a few. Fenton's creative skills and delicate colors make their products most desirable. Fenton produced no crackle glass until 1992 and 1993.

This information was furnished to me by the Fenton Museum through the article written in the *Glass Collector's Digest*, "The Fenton Story" by Alan Linn. Through the Fenton Art Glass Collectors of America's Williamstown, West Virginia, branch office, I was able to obtain pictures of the crackle glass manufactured from the 1992 and 1993 Fenton catalog. These catalogs show three basic items produced in blue, pink, and green iridescent colors. (Detailed descriptions can be found in the manufacturer's identification guidelines.)

Pink Iridescent Fenton Basket carrying the newest addition to
our family, "Precious," my daughter's new seven-week-old
Himalayan kitten.

Hamon Glass
Scott Depot, West Virginia

Kanawha Glass Specialties, Inc.
Kanawha Glass Company
Dunbar, West Virginia

Williamsburg Glass Company
Lightfoot, Virginia

Raymond Dereume Glass Company
Punxsutawney, Pennsylvania

Hamon Glass was founded by Robert Hamon in 1932. Hamon produced crackle glass from 1950 until 1970. (For the shapes and colors, please see the manufacturer's identification guidelines.)

Hamon glass was purchased by Keith Merritt of Kanawha Glass Company in 1969. Hamon pieces produced from 1969 until 1980 carry a Kanawha label.

Crackle glass is no longer being produced at Hamon Glass, but I was told that "Mr. Hamon will make you a piece of crackle glass today if you catch him on a good day."

I have no piece of Hamon glass with a label, but Mr. Hamon described his two labels to me. The first Hamon label was a one-half inch pink strip with the name DIANA written in blue. These labels came into existence in 1950 soon after the birth of his first child, Diana. In later years, a label in the shape of West Virginia carrying the name Hamon across it was used, also used was a silver label with a green glass blower carrying a Hamon name.

D. P. Merritt, 1894-1982, was the founding father of Kanawha Glass Company. In 1909 at age fifteen, D. P. Merritt learned hand cutting at Huntington Cut Tumbler, Huntington, West Virginia. His first job was with Cambridge Bottle between 1909 and 1915. Mr. Merritt worked as a cutter for Fenton Glass of Williamstown, West Virginia, in 1915; for Cambridge Glass of Cambridge, Ohio, in 1917 (also serving as a designer there); for Lancaster Glass of Lancaster, Ohio, in 1919; and New Martinsville Glass of New Martinsville, West Virginia, in 1922.

In 1924 Mr. Merritt established his own cutting shop in Dunbar, West Virginia. In 1927 Mr. Meritt and Dunbar Glass merged and he became foreman of the cutting department at Dunbar Glass in Dunbar, West Virginia. In 1938 Mr. Merritt had worked his way to the General Superintendent of all productions at Dunbar Glass. He remained there until he retired in 1952.

Kanahwa Glass Company adopted its name from the surrounding county and the river which flows nearby and derived its name from a small tribe of Indians who once dwelt upon its banks. Their tribal name has been spelled many ways, ranging from Conoys and Connois to Kanawha.

Kanawha Glass was started in 1954, when a group of former Dunbar Glass employees requested that D. P. Merritt establish a small shop where they could cut or decorate purchased glass. The shop was located on the outskirts of Dunbar, West Virginia, in a rented building and was incorporated as Kanawha Glass Specialties, Inc., on September 3, 1954.

Within a year a location was purchased and a plant built in West Dunbar, West Virginia. Construction was aided by labor supplied by the glass workers. In 1955, this plant started producing hand blown crystal glass pitchers and continued to cut or decorate purchased glass which was sold with the pitchers as beverage and juice sets. These sets were sold through national distributors in New York City under their brand names.

On April 26, 1957, the company name was changed to Kanawha Glass Company, and in 1958 Kanawha produced its first crackled glass items for Robinson Clay Products of Akron, Ohio. They were pitchers and vases in crystal, copper blue, and a light amber. In 1959 Kanawha Glass introduced a larger line of colored and crystal crackled glass to be sold by its own sales representatives. Sales coverage eventually became national, and production grew to four hand blown and one hand pressed shops in the next four years.

The controlling interest of Hamon Handcrafted Glass, Scott Depot, West Virginia, was purchased by Kanawha Glass in 1969. Ruby crackled glass items from the Scott Depot plant were incorporated into the Kanawha line. Because each plant had its own capabilities, production was allotted between the plants based on their efficiency. Although the vast majority of crackled glass was still produced by Kanawha in West Dunbar, three hand blown shops were employed full time in Scott Depot.

Williamsburg Pottery in Lightfoot, Virginia, and Kanawha Glass established "Williamsburg Glass," as a small show plant which was opened in the summer of 1971 in the Pottery complex. However, natural gas curtailment effectively stopped that effort, and the Kanawha Glass holdings in Williamsburg Glass were sold to the Pottery. Only a few crackled glass items were produced there. These items were made from the Kanawha molds.

This Willamsburg company is sometimes confused with work done by the Blenko Company for Colonial Williamsburg from 1941 until 1961. These pieces were made for the "Colonial Williamsburg Reproduction" line. Blenko used a green label on these pieces with "C.W." initials in the center. Williamsburg Glass Company used a black label that read "Hand Made Glass, Williamsburg Glass Company."

In March of 1974 Kanawha Glass acquired the machinery, equipment, and molds of Shelby Earl Glass Company in Huntington, West Virginia. The equipment was moved to the Kanawha plant in West Dunbar, and Kanawha Glass began the production of communion glasses.

On November 8, 1975, D. P. Merritt resigned as president of Kanawha Glass. He was succeeded by his son, Keith C. Merritt. After his resignation, Mr. Merritt continued at Kanawha until he retired at the age of eighty-six.

During the natural gas curtailment from about 1974 to 1978, the ability to produce glass suffered greatly. Kanawha could only run for a period of seven months a year during that time. Natural gas prices increased tremendously, causing glass prices to soar. Imports were able to attract customers while domestic plants could not produce; or later, when they could, they could not compete with low import prices. The decline in the market for domestic glass caused the closing of the Scott Depot plant in January of 1980.

Kanawha Glass continued in production until June of 1987, when, because of management's desire to divest itself of ownership, the plant, real estate, molds, machinery, and equipment were sold to Raymond Dereume Glass, Inc., of Punxsutawney, Pennsylvania. The machinery and equipment were moved to Punxsutawney, where they are now used. Keith C. Merritt, the president at the closing of Kanawha, served as a consultant to Raymond Dereume Glass, Inc., until 1991, when he moved to Arizona.

Raymond Dereume, originally of Belgium, began a sheet glass, import export business in 1921. In 1945 his son August Dereume joined his father. Together they continued the manufacturing of sheet glass. In 1975 Raymond Dereume died, and his grandson, August (Jack) Dereume, Jr., joined his father in this family business. A year later, the father-son operation added pressed and blown glass to their production line. In 1985 Jack's father passed away, and he eventually dropped the sheet glass line and concentrated on the most popular production of pressed and blown glass.

In 1987 Dereume Glass Company bought the Kanawha Glass Company out of Dunbar, West Virginia. For two years the production of the last Kanawha glass line was produced, including crackle glass. Realizing the Kanawha glass line and the Dereume glass line were more than the limited staff at Dereume Glass Company could handle, Mr. Dereume decided to drop the Kanawha line in 1989.

Jack Dereume continues in his operation at the Raymond Dereume Glass Company. The Dereume glass line includes only two items in the crackle glass. (See manufacturer's identification guidelines for detailed description. The Dereume line consists primarily of pressed and blown church and restaurant supply candle related items.

KANAWHA GLASS COMPANY

Kanawha 1966 and 1973 Catalog Pages
(These pages only represent a small percentage of crackle glass produced by Kanawha Glass Company)

1966 Kanawha Catalog pages 2, 3, 5, 6 & 7, 10, 11, 12.

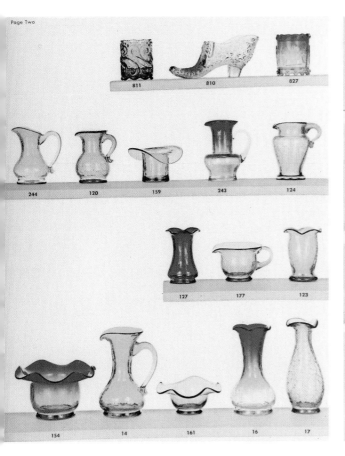

811 810 827

244 120 159 243 124

127 177 123

154 14 161 16 17

Kanawha

194 131 157

130 195 193 187 188

126 122 160

186 15 158 125 153

Kanawha

213 224 214 820 192

212 236 221 220 230 227

204 225 228 168 148 229 819

73

Kanawha

93   207   92

199   6-8H

96   95   216

179   174   46H

206   6-8   176   197

Kanawha

233   7   31

240   87

42   38   86   149   88

1973 Kanwaha Catalog, page 6

1973 Kanwaha Catalog, page 28, showing the ruby red pieces of crackle glass that will carry a Kanawha label, although they were created by Hamon Glass Company employees.

1973 Kanwaha Catalog, page 26

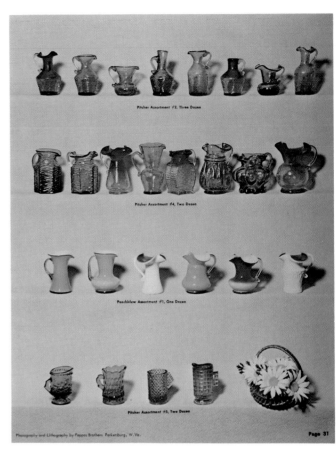

1973 Kanwaha Catalog, page 30

1973 Kanwaha Catalog, page 31

1973 Kanwaha Catalog, pages 4, 7, 9, 16, 17, and 29

Animal Assortment #4, Two Dozen

Animal Assortment #6, One Dozen

Vase Assortment #1, Three Dozen

Animal Assortment #5, One Dozen

A display of Kanawha's superb craftsmanship.

Kanawha's beautiful art work on display.

Kanawha's amberina pieces are popular with collectors.

Kanawha's large variety of colors, shapes, and styles.

Yellow/amber Satin glass #241 Kanawha Pitcher, very rare, 1973, H. 5.25". Value $50-$75.

Yellow #177 Kanawha miniature creamer, 1959-1987, H. 3.25". *Courtesy of Jane and Donald Thompson.* Value $15-$20.

Amber Kanawha miniature pitcher, 1959-1987, H. 3.25". *Courtesy of Jane and Donald Thompson.* Value $15-$20.

Amberina assortment #1 Kanawha miniature pitcher, 1959-1987, H. 3.75". *Courtesy of Dana Noggle.* Value $20-$25.

Amberina assortment #2 Kanawha miniature pitcher, 1959-1987, H. 3.5". *Courtesy of Dana Noggle.* Value $20-$25.

Amberina #179 Kanawha pitcher, 1966, H. 6". Value $35-$45.

Amberina assortment #4 Kanawha miniature pitcher, 1973, H. 4.25". Value $25-$35.

Amberina #264 Kanawha pitcher, 1959-1987, H. 4.5". *Courtesy of Jane and Donald Thompson.* Value $25-$35.

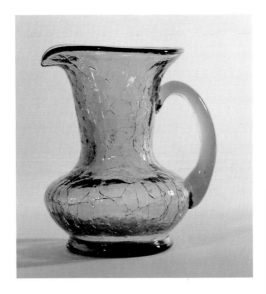

Green assortment #1 Kanawha miniature pitcher, 1959-1987, H. 4". Value $20-$25.

Orange amberina #46 Kanawha pitcher, 1959-1987, H. 6". Value $40-$50.

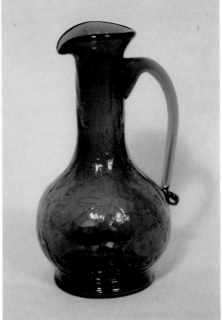

Amethyst #21 Kanawha oil and vinegar pitcher, 1959-1987, H. 6". Value $45-$55.

Bright yellow #240 Kanawha miniature pitcher, 1959-1987, H. 8". Value $35-$45.

Amberina #220 Kanawha miniature pitcher, 1959-1987, H. 4". Value $25-$35.

Brown #21 Kanawha oil and vinegar pitcher, 1959-1987, H. 6". Value $40-$50.

Amberina #38 Kanawha pencil vase, 1966, H. 18". *Courtesy of Jane and Donald Thompson.* Value $40-$50.

Orange amberina Kanawha miniature pitcher, 1959-1987, H. 3.25". *Courtesy of Pat Paschall.* Value $20-$25.

Yellow Kanawha vase, 1959-1987, H. 13". *Courtesy of Jane and Donald Thompson.* Value $30-$40.

Green #221 Kanawha miniature vase, 1959-1987, H. 3.5". *Courtesy of Pat Paschall.* Value $15-$20.

Yellow buttercup #38 Kanawha pencil vase, 1966, H. 18". *Courtesy of Jane and Donald Thompson.* Value $35-$45.

Amberina Kanawha vase, 1959-1987, H. 4.5". Value $20-$25.

HAMON GLASS COMPANY

Display of Hamon's beautiful colors and craftsmanship.

For a period Hamon's ruby red pieces appeared in Kanawha catalogs. The two outside pieces are Hamon and the center piece is Kanawha's #390 vase.

Blue #1138 Hamon pitcher, 1950-1970, H. 7.5". Value $35-$45.

Ruby red #1138 Hamon pitcher, 1950-1970, H. 6.25". Value $40-$50.

Amberina #1128 Hamon pitcher, 1950-1970, H. 5.25". Value $30-$40.

Ruby red #1128 Hamon pitcher, 1950-1970, H. 5.25". Value $30-$40.

Orange amberina Hamon pitcher, 1950-1970, H. 5". Value $25-35.

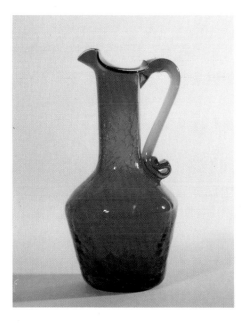

Red amberina Hamon pitcher, 1950-1970, H. 5.5". Value $30-$40

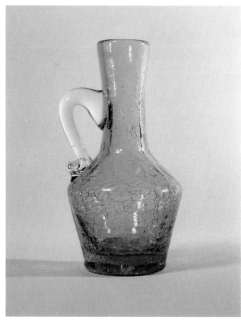

Amber #1123 Hamon jug, 1950-1970, H. 5.5". *Courtesy of Jane and Donald Thompson.* Value $15-$20.

Emerald green Hamon vase with applied neck decoration, 1950-1970, H. 7". *Courtesy of Jane and Donald Thompson,* $45-$55.

Amberina #1123 Hamon jug, 1950-1970, H. 5". Value $20-$30.

Light blue Hamon vase with applied neck decoration, 1950-1970, H. 5.75". *Courtesy of Lucille Holcomb.* Value $45-$55.

Amberina Hamon pitcher, 1950-1970, H. 6". Value $40-$50.

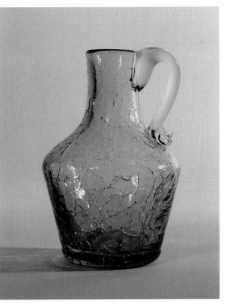

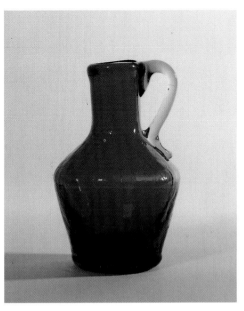

Green #1124 Hamon jug, 1950-1970, H. 4.5". *Courtesy of Jane and Donald Thompson.* Value $15-$20.

Green #1124 Hamon jug, 1950-1970, H. 4". *Courtesy of Jane and Donald Thompson.* Value $15-$20.

Ruby red Hamon jug, 1950-1970, H. 4". Value $20-$25.

WILLIAMSBURG GLASS COMPANY

All three pieces here were made from the same Kanawha mold, represented L-R: Williamsburg, Kanawha, and Dereume.

Cranberry Williamsburg miniature pitcher, rare color, Kanawha mold #6-8H, mid 1970s, H. 8.25". Value $50-$75.

Tri-State Glass Manufacturing Company
Huntington, West Virginia

Pilgrim Glass Corporation
Huntington, West Virginia
Ceredo, West Virginia

Alfred Knobler, the founding father of the Pilgrim Glass Company out of Ceredo, West Virginia, graduated from Virginia Tech with a degree in Ceramic Engineering. After graduation he went to work for Trenton Potteries in New Jersey until World War II demanded his time be given to the War Department.

After the war, Mr. Knobler opened his own business, buying from glass and pottery factories and selling to retail outlets. One of Mr. Knobler's suppliers was Tri-State Glass Manufacturing Company in Huntington, West Virginia, owned and operated by Walter Bailey.

Mr. Bailey's Tri-State Glass plant was struggling because of a problem with the gas pressure. He didn't have enough gas to run his furnace at the required temperature for melting glass. Mr. Bailey approached Mr. Knobler and asked if he would consider buying this company from him. Mr. Knobler, after working out a solution to the problem with the Columbus Gas Company, agreed to purchase Mr. Bailey's business.

Crackle glass was the main product produced from 1949 until 1969. This spectacular glassware was produced in many shapes and a variety of vibrant colors. However, by 1970 crackle glass had just about run its course, and the demand was so small it was discontinued from the product line.

Although crackle glass is no longer being produced by the Pilgrim Glass Company, the company is still in operation today and Pilgrim continues to have many success stories in the glass industry...one of which is its magnificent cameo glass.

Pilgrim's exquisite art work.

Three Pilgrim miniature pitchers in tangerine, ruby red, and olive green.

A display of Pilgrim's vibrant colors and superb craftsmanship.

Pilgrim made a large variety of miniature pitchers in different shapes, colors, and handle styles.

Pilgrim items with clear handles were manufactured after the early 1960s, when crystal handles were put on the line.

Pilgrim handles that were the same color of the item produced
were manufactured prior to the early 1960s.

These Pilgrim miniature pitchers display a variety of colors,
styles, and shapes.

Pilgrim miniature pitchers in a variety of shapes, colors, and
different handle styles.

Pilgrim made a left-handed miniature pitcher in different styles and colors.

The left-handed Pilgrim miniature pitchers were made in the same shape as regular pitchers.

Pilgrim vases are many times found with applied neck decorations.

Pilgrim Pitchers with Colored Handles

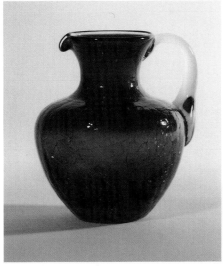

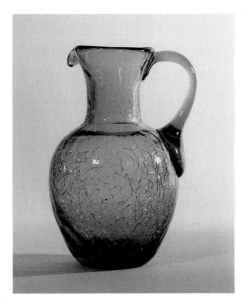

Green #767 Pilgrim miniature pitcher, 1949-1959, H. 4.5". Value $20-$25.

Ruby red #759 Pilgrim miniature pitcher, 1949-1959, H. 3.5". Value $20-$25.

Tangerine #757 Pilgrim miniature pitcher, 1949-1959, H. 3.5". *Courtesy of Dana Noggle.* Value $20-$25.

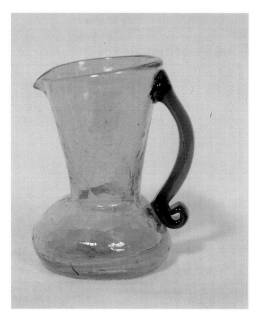

Yellow #748 Pilgrim miniature pitcher
with a green handle, 1949-1959, H. 4".
Value $25-$30.

Ruby red Pilgrim miniature pitcher,
1949-1959, H. 4". Value $25-$30.

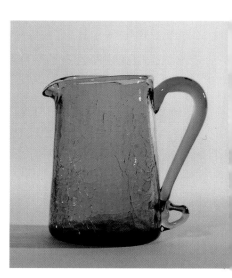

Blue Pilgrim miniature pitcher, 1949-
1959, H. 4". Value $20-$25.

Ruby red #760 Pilgrim miniature pitcher,
marked, 1949-1959, H. 5". Value $30-$40.

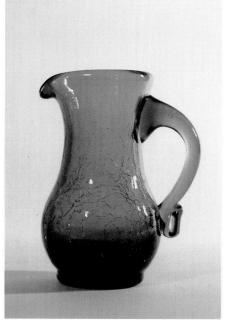

Green Pilgrim miniature pitcher, 1949-
1959, H. 3". Value $15-$20.

Green Pilgrim miniature pitcher, 1949-
1959, H. 2.5". *Courtesy of Jane and Donald
Thompson.* Value $15-$20.

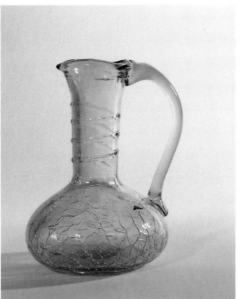

Amber Pilgrim pitcher, 1949-1959, H. 5.25". Value $25-$35.

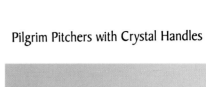

Pilgrim Pitchers with Crystal Handles

Light green Pilgrim creamer, 1949-1959, H. 3". Value $15-$20.

Olive green Pilgrim pitcher, 1960-1969, H. 5.5". Value $20-$25.

Green Pilgrim pitcher, 1949-1959, H. 4.5". Value $20-$25.

Blue Pilgrim pitcher, 1949-1959, H. 5". *Courtesy of Jane and Donald Thompson.* Value $25-$30.

Tangerine #748 Pilgrim pitcher, 1960-1969, H. 5.5". Value $25-$35.

95

Ruby red #748 Pilgrim pitcher, 1960-1969, H. 5.5". Value $25-$35.

Olive green group C Pilgrim pitcher, 1960-1969, H. 6.75". Value $20-$25.

Light blue Pilgrim miniature pitcher, 1960-1969, H. 3.5". Value $15-$20.

Amber group B Pilgrim pitcher, 1960-1969, H. 4.75". Value $15-$20.

Olive green #753 Pilgrim miniature pitcher, 1960-1969, H. 4.75". Value $15-$20.

Lemon/green Pilgrim miniature pitcher, 1960-1969, H. 4". Value $15-$20.

96

Amber #749 Pilgrim left-handed miniature pitcher, 1960-1969, H. 3.5". Value
$15-$20.

Ruby red #748 Pilgrim miniature pitcher
with ridged handle, 1960-1969, H. 3.5".
Value $20-$25.

Blue #748 Pilgrim left-handed miniature
pitcher, 1960-1969, H. 3.5". *Courtesy of
Dana Noggle.* Value $15-$20.

Ruby red #770 Pilgrim miniature pitcher,
1960-1969, H. 4". *Courtesy of Jane and
Donald Thompson.* Value $20-$25.

Olive green Pilgrim miniature pitcher,
1960-1969, H. 4". Value $15-$20.

Green #748 Pilgrim miniature pitcher,
1960-1969, H. 3.5". Value $10-$15.

Blue #770 Pilgrim miniature pitcher,
1960-1969, H. 4". *Courtesy of Jane and
Donald Thompson.* Value $15-$20.

Amber Pilgrim miniature pitcher, 1960-1969, H. 3.5". Value $10-$15.

Amber #750 Pilgrim miniature pitcher with ridged handle, 1960-1969, H. 4". *Courtesy of Jane and Donald Thompson.* Value $20-$25.

Tangerine Pilgrim miniature pitcher, 1960-1969, H. 4.5". Value $20-$25.

Amber #750 Pilgrim miniature pitcher, 1960-1969, H. 3.75". Value $10-$15.

Olive green #750 Pilgrim left-handed miniature pitcher, 1960-1969, H. 4". Value $20-$25.

Lemon/green Pilgrim miniature pitcher, 1960-1969, H. 4". *Courtesy of Dana Noggle.* Value $15-$20.

Olive green Pilgrim miniature pitcher, 1960-1969, H. 4.25". *Courtesy of Lucille Holcomb.* Value $20-$25.

Tangerine Pilgrim miniature pitcher, 1960-1969, H. 4.5". Value $20-$25.

Green Pilgrim miniature pitcher, 1960-1969, H. 4.5". Value $15-$20.

Ruby red #759 Pilgrim pitcher, 1960-1969, H. 5.25". *Courtesy of Dana Noggle.* Value $25-$35.

Tangerine #752 Pilgrim miniature pitcher, 1960-1969, H. 4.5". *Courtesy of Dana Noggle.* Value $20-$25.

Amber #606 Pilgrim benedictine, 1960-1969, H. 4". *Courtesy of Dana Noggle.* Value $20-$25.

Tangerine #757 Pilgrim left-handed pitcher, 1960-1969, H. 3.5".
Value $20-$25.

Ruby red #756 Pilgrim miniature pitcher with ridged handle, 1960-1969, H. 4.75". *Courtesy of Dana Noggle.* Value $25-$35.

Brown #748 Pilgrim miniature pitcher, 1960-1969, H. 4.25". Value $25-$35.

Ruby red #756 Pilgrim miniature pitcher, 1960-1969. H. 4.75". *Courtesy of Pat Paschall.* Value $20-$25.

Amber #754 Pilgrim miniature pitcher, 1960-1969, H. 4.5". Value $15-$20.

Ruby red Pilgrim miniature pitcher with ridged handle, 1960-1969, H. 4.75". *Courtesy of Dana Noggle.* Value $25-$35.

Tangerine #769 Pilgrim miniature pitcher, 1960-1969, H. 3.5".
Value $15-$20.

Ruby red #769 Pilgrim miniature pitcher, 1960-1969, H. 3.75".
Courtesy of Dana Noggle. Value $15-$20.

Amber #769 Pilgrim miniature pitcher with ridged handle, 1960-
1969, H. 3.5". Value $15-$20.

Amber #769 Pilgrim left-handed miniature pitcher, 1960-1969,
H. 3.5". Value $15-$20.

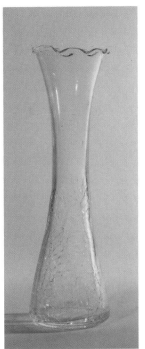

Clear Pilgrim vase, 1949-1969, H. 5".
Value $15-$20.

Green Pilgrim vase, 1949-1969, H. 4.5". *Courtesy of Jane and Donald Thompson.* Value $15-$20.

Two-tone amber and brown Pilgrim bottle, 1949-1979, H. 15.25". Value $25-$35.

Two amber Pilgrim vases, left vase, marked, 1949-1969, H. 4.5". *Courtesy of Jane and Donald Thompson.* Value L: $20-$25, R: $15-$20.

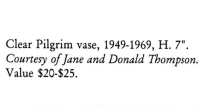

Clear Pilgrim vase, 1949-1969, H. 7". *Courtesy of Jane and Donald Thompson.* Value $20-$25.

Light green fluted Pilgrim vase with applied neck decoration, 1949-1969, H. 7.5". Value $25-$35.

Yellow Pilgrim vase with applied neck decoration, 1949-1969, H. 6". *Courtesy of Dana Noggle.* Value $25-$35.

Brown Pilgrim vase with applied rope, 1949-1969, H. 7". *Courtesy of Jane and Donald Thompson.* Value $25-$35.

Yellow Pilgrim vase with applied rope, 1949-1969, H. 7.5". *Courtesy of Jane and Donald Thompson.* Value $25-$35.

Blue Pilgrim vase with applied neck decoration, marked, 1949-1969, H. 7.25". *Courtesy of Dana Noggle.* Value $25-$35.

Olive green Pilgrim vase (or possibly a water jar with the cup missing), 1949-1969, H. 6.5". Value $20-$25.

Green #71 Pilgrim pinched vase, 1949-1969, H. 4.5". Value $15-$20.

Pilgrim Jugs With Crystal Handles

Amber #755 Pilgrim jug, marked, 1960-1969, H. 4". *Courtesy of Jane and Donald Thompson.* Value $20-$25.

Amber group C Pilgrim vase, 1949-1969, H. 6.5". Value $20-$25.

Ruby red #755 Pilgrim jug, marked, 1960-1969, H. 4.25". *Courtesy of Dana Noggle.* Value $25-$35.

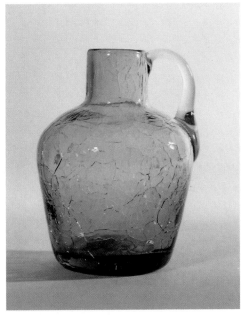

Lemon/green #755 Pilgrim jug, marked, 1960-1969, H. 3.75". Value $20-$25.

Light amber Pilgrim jug, 1960-1969, H. 6". *Courtesy of Jane and Donald Thompson.* Value $15-$20.

Ruby red Pilgrim long-neck jug, 1960-1969, H. 4.25". *Courtesy of Pat Paschall*. Value $25-$35.

The Rainbow Art Company
Huntington, West Virginia

The Rainbow Art Glass Company
Huntington, West Virginia

Viking Glass Company
(New Martinsville, West Virginia)
Huntington, West Virginia

I was most fortunate to be able to contact Paul Kilgore who worked as the manager of The Rainbow Art Glass Company for some forty years. Mr. Kilgore put me in touch with Henry Manus, one of the original owners of The Rainbow Art Glass Company, and I spoke with Mr. Manus and Emmy, his wife, at length.

Before the Rainbow Art Company ever came to be, a Mrs. Leopold and a Mr. Foster began hand painting glassware in a loft in Long Island, New York. Three months later their business was taken over by Henry Manus and Jo Goudeket, who years later became Mr. Manus' father-in-law as well as business partner when Henry married Emmy. Both Mr. Manus and Mr. Goudeket were from Amsterdam, Holland, although they had not met each other prior to coming to the United States.

This new-found business took off, and in a very short time they had moved from a loft into a second location. Soon these two locations were too small, and in 1942 they were contacted by Dr. W. S. Rosenheim, then manager of the Chamber of Commerce in Huntington, about purchasing an empty building in his town. They were tempted by the fact that Huntington would offer cheap and abundant fuel gas, a convenient supply of materials used in glass manufacture, skilled labor, and other attractive advantages, so they decided to accept Dr. Rosenheim's offer. They loaded up two railroad freight cars and moved to Huntington to occupy a factory twenty times bigger than their two locations in New York. This is where The Rainbow Art Company, under the ownership of Joseph Goudeket and Henry Manus, began its long and successful years in the glass industry.

This same building had been the home of Bonita Art Glass Company, formerly of Wheeling, West Virginia. Otto Jaeger, manager of Bonita, discontinued business there around 1939. Although they left this building, further records provided to me by Dean Six show a Bonita Glass Company of Huntington, West Virginia, advertising their "Robert P. Pierce" line of glassware. Bonita offered fourteen items in crackle glass. (See manufacturer's identification guidelines.)

Paul Kilgore joined the Rainbow Art team in 1948 as their plant manager. At the time Mr. Kilgore joined The Rainbow Art Company, they did not produce glass but instead decorated crystal glass pieces purchased from other companies. This was done from 1942 until 1954.

In 1954 Mr. Goudeket passed away, and Henry and Emmy Manus continued the operations. Shortly after the death of Emmy's father the name of the business was changed to the Rainbow Art Glass Company, and production of Rainbow's "hand blown glass" began. After Mr. Goudeket's death, Mr. Manus said "Paul Kilgore is the man I could and did rely on. We could not have done it without Paul."

Rainbow's hand blown art was exquisite, with stoppers sometimes measuring longer than the pieces themselves. From 1954 until 1980 crackle glass was being produced in ten radiant colors. (See the manufacturer's identification guidelines for colors.)

In 1973 the Viking Glass Company purchased the plant and continued operations until the plant burned in 1983. Mr. Kilgore of Rainbow stayed with the plant under the Viking management. In 1980, three years before the plant burned, a decision was made to return to the decoration of glass rather than the production of glass. Therefore, 1979 was the last year crackle glass was produced by the Viking Glass Company out of Huntington, West Virginia.

The original Rainbow label was fan shaped with silver background and black lettering. This was the true Rainbow trademark used in the beginning years of Rainbow's production of hand blown glass. Years later, labels in the shape of a glass bubble were used in silver and black for the wholesale pieces and silver and red for the seconds that were going to their retail store which was managed by Mrs. Emmy Manus.

Although the original Rainbow Art Glass Company is no longer in business, their contributions to the glass industry will live on in the homes and hearts of all the Rainbow collectors of the world. Mr. and Mrs. Manus are enjoying a well deserved retirement in Florida, although retirement to Mr. Manus finds him extremely involved in "worthwhile civic organizations." Even though he carries the nickname of "Poof" in Florida, he will forever be known as "Mr. Rainbow" to me.

Old Rainbow Catalog Pages
These pages only represent a small percentage of crackle glass
produced by the Rainbow Art Glass Company.

Old Rainbow catalog, pages 1, 12 & 13

Rainbow catalog showing various candleholder and pitcher styles, page 8.

Rainbow catalog showing different vase styles, page 9.

Rainbow catalog showing different styles of cruets, page 10.

Rainbow catalog showing a variety of ruby red styles, pages 14 & 15.

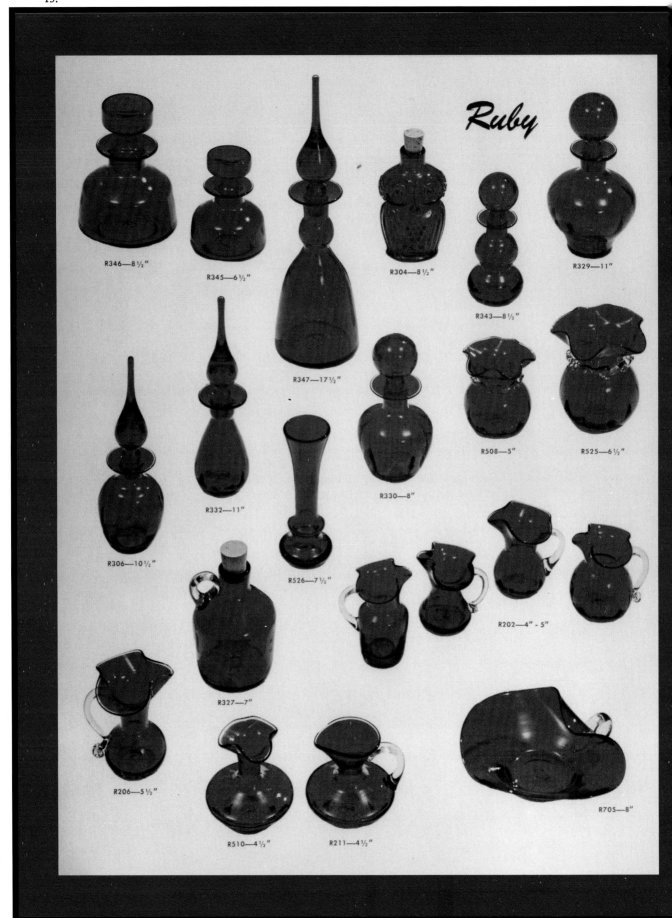

Ruby

R346—8½"

R345—6½"

R347—17½"

R304—8½"

R343—8½"

R329—11"

R306—10½"

R332—11"

R526—7½"

R330—8"

R508—5"

R525—6½"

R327—7"

R202—4"-5"

R206—5½"

R510—4½"

R211—4½"

R705—8"

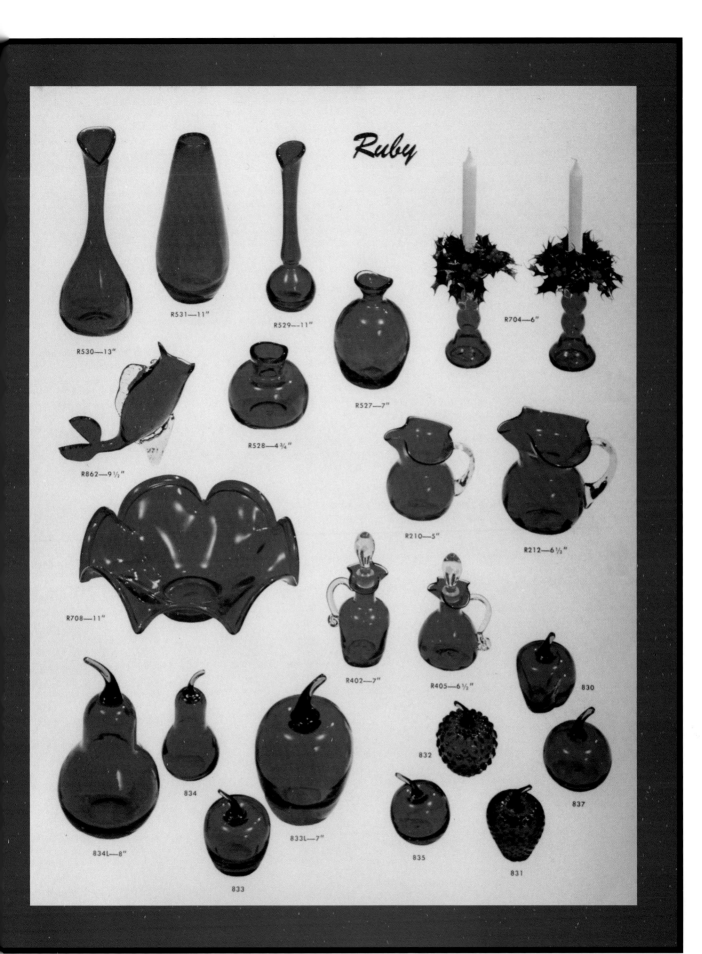

Ruby

R530—13"

R531—11"

R529—11"

R527—7"

R704—6"

R862—9½"

R528—4¾"

R708—11"

R210—5"

R212—6½"

R402—7"

R405—6½"

830

832

837

834

834L—8"

833L—7"

835

831

833

Rainbow's variety of styles come in different radiant colors.

Rainbow catalog showing bathroom boutique styles, page 11.

These three Rainbow pitchers have the same mouth and handle
styles, although they vary in size and body shape.

The first two Rainbow pitchers have the same mouth and handle styles and the last two have the same body style. By mixing the body, mouth, and handle styles, different looks can be achieved.

A display of Rainbow's exquisite craftsmanship in brilliant Rainbow colors and unique styles.

Two amberina Rainbow vases with different mouth styles, 1954-1973, H. 5.5". *Courtesy of Pat Paschall.* Value $80-$100 (set).

This cranberry Rainbow pitcher was hand painted, very rare, 1954-1973, H. 5". Value $25-$35.

These three ruby red Rainbow vases, although different in size and shape, have the exact same mouth style.

Two turquoise #201 Rainbow miniature pitchers, 1954-1973, H. 3.5". *Courtesy of Dana Noggle.* Value $40-$50 (set).

Amber #201 Rainbow miniature pitcher, 1954-1973, H. 4". Value $15-$20.

Orange amberina #201 Rainbow miniature pitcher, 1954-1973, H. 3.5". Value $20-$25.

Ruby red #201 Rainbow miniature pitcher, 1954-1973, H. 3.5". *Courtesy of Jane and Donald Thompson.* Value $20-$25.

Amber Rainbow pitcher, 1954-1973, H. 5.25". Value $30-$40.

Orange amberina #201 Rainbow miniature pitcher, 1954-1973, H. 3.75". Value $20-$25.

Turquoise Rainbow Pitcher, 1954-1973, H. 5.25". Value $30-$40.

Turquoise Rainbow pitcher, 1954-1973, H. 5". Value $30-$40.

Orange amberina #202 Rainbow pitcher, 1954-1973, H. 4.5". *Courtesy of Dana Noggle.* Value $25-$35.

Dark red amberina Rainbow pitcher (only piece I have ever found with a red handle), 1954-1973, H. 5". Value $35-$45.

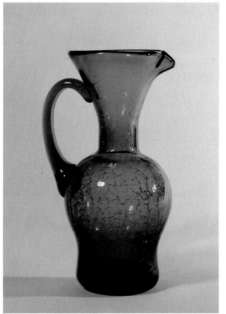

Olive green Rainbow pitcher, 1954-1973, H. 8". *Courtesy of Jane and Donald Thompson.* Value $40-$50.

Amberina Rainbow pitcher, 1954-1973, H. 7". *Courtesy of Jane and Donald Thompson.* Value $50-$75.

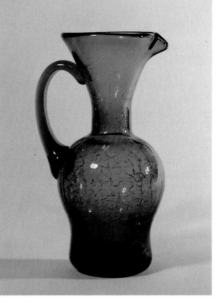

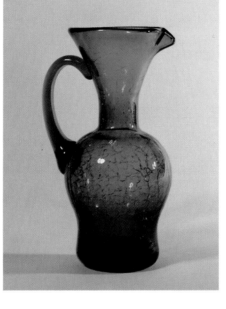

Amber #202 Rainbow pitcher, 1954-1973, H. 5". Value $25-$35.

Blue Rainbow vase, 1954-1973, H. 2.5".
Value $10-$15.

Amberina #525 Rainbow vase with
applied neck decoration, 1954-1973, H.
6". Value $50-$75.

Ruby red Rainbow pinched vase, 1954-
1973, H. 5". *Courtesy of Jane and Donald
Thompson.* Value $30-$40.

Ruby red Rainbow pitcher, 1954-1973, H.
7". *Courtesy of Jane and Donald Thompson.* Value $50-$75.

Amberina Rainbow vase, 1954-1973, H.
5.5". *Courtesy of Dana Noggle.* Value $30-
$40.

Ruby red #504 Rainbow vase, 1954-1973,
H. 7.5". Value $40-$50.

Ruby red Rainbow pitcher, 1954-1973, H.
7". Value $50-$75.

Ruby red Rainbow vase, 1954-1973, H.
5". Value $30-$40.

Turquoise green Rainbow vase with fluted mouth, 1954-1973, H. 5". Value $30-$40.

Blue #6021 Rainbow vase, 1954-1973, H. 5". Value $25-$35.

Olive green Rainbow vase, 1954-1973, H. 4.5". Value $15-$20.

Amber #504 Rainbow vase with applied neck decoration, 1954-1973, H. 5". *Courtesy of Jane and Donald Thompson.* Value $25-35.

Clear Rainbow pinched vase (Rainbow crystal is very clear), 1954-1973, H. 4.25". Value $15-$20.

Ruby red Rainbow vase, 1954-1973, H. 4". *Courtesy of Pat Paschall.* Value $20-$25.

VIKING GLASS COMPANY

Blue #27 Viking 7" ashtray. Value $30-$40.

Amber #27 Viking 7" ashtray. Value $30-$40.

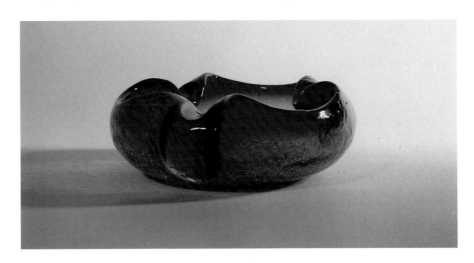

Amberina #27 Viking 7" ashtray. Value $35-$45.

Manufacturer's
Identification Guidelines
1930s-1990s

Bischoff produced:
1) Regular and "alligator" crackles
2) Medium and large crackles
3) Unusual pieces (some look European)
4) Many green and amber pieces in window sill size
5) Glass that appeared thicker and heavier
6) Colors: gold, copperette, poinsettia red, wisteria, lime, peacock blue, orange, amethyst, crystal

Blenko produced or produces:
1) Crackle glass from around 1946 to the present
2) Small, medium, and large crackled pieces
3) Free form hand blown pieces with pontil mark
4) Smooth finished pontil marks on most pieces
5) Too many colors to name (all colors)
6) Many very large pieces
7) Pieces with applied rosettes, leaves, and many other decorations
8) Many pinched and crimped vases
9) Large decanters with crackled stoppers
10) Some pieces that can be identified by shape or style in the *Blenko Glass 1930-53* book by Eason Eige and Rick Wilson
11) Very few miniature pieces
12) A few marked pieces 1959-60
13) Labels with the open hand and Blenko written under it were used until the mid-1980s
14) Colonial Williamsburg Reproductions and used a green label that read "Williamsburg Restoration" until 1965
15) Crackle glass most likely beginning in the 1940 as it was not listed in their catalogs until 1946

Dereume produced:
1) "Kanawha mold" crackle glass from 1988-1989
2) Crackle glass until present
3) These crackle glass pieces only at the present time:
   a. Candle cylinder used mostly in churches
      1. Colors: clear, dark blue, amber, and purple
   b. Candle globes used mostly in restaurants
      1. Colors: clear, ruby, and vintage (amberina)

Fenton produced:
1) Crackle glass in 1992 and 1993
2) Large and medium crackles only

3) Mold blown only
4) Three iridescent colors: Blue, Pink, Green
5) Items produced in 1992:
   1. Green "Sea Mist" Iridescent
      a. 14.5" vase
      b. 14" vase
      c. 10.5" fluted vase
      d. 10.5" pitcher with pulled handle
      e. 11" fluted basket with decorative handle
   2. Blue "Twilight Crackle" Iridescent
      a. Five items (same as green)
   3. Pink Iridescent
      a. Five items (same as green except the 14" vase is fluted in the pink)
6) Items produced in 1993:
   1. Large 14.5" vase was retired in all colors
   2. 10.5" pitcher was retired in all colors
   3. Blue and Pink Iridescent made other three pieces named in 1992 for their colors
   4. Green picked up all new styles, six items
      a. 3 fluted vases
      b. 1 vase
      c. 1 pitcher with drop over handle
      d. 1 fluted basket with plain handle
7) Produced only large pieces

Hamon produced:
1) Crackle glass from 1950-1970 (They merged with Kanawha in 1966, but continued to operate under both names...each using their own techniques.)
2) Only small crackles
3) Free form hand blown crackle glass
4) Mold blown with applied pontil mark
5) Bottoms that are never smooth
6) Colors: crystal, blue, green, lavender, ruby, amber, and amberina
7) Pulled handles usually extend from the top of the piece and look like a "question mark"
8) Handles were almost always crystal
9) Spouts on their pitchers usually make a distinct dip at the nose
10) Most pieces seem a little heavier when compared with other manufactured pieces the same size
11) Most popular items are pitchers, tumblers (glasses), bowls, some stemmed glasses, and vases
12) Three labels:
   1. One-half inch strip that read Diana

(Mr. Hamon's first born child), pink with blue writing
2. Shaped like West Virginia and reads "Hamon"
3. Silver with green and black with a glass blower and the Hamon name

Heritage produced:
1) Small crackles
2) Free form hand blown pieces
3) Color: Orange (only color I have seen, I'm sure there are many more)

Kanawha produced:
1) Crackle glass from 1957-1987
2) Fine crackle (mostly)
3) Mold blown pieces most often with seams
4) Bottoms always smooth
5) Colors: bright yellow, dark amber, red, amberina, purple, brown, yellow/green, blue, green, cranberry
6) Mostly colored handles
7) Labels are black with gold letters that spell Kanawha

Kanawha/Hamon Glass Company:
1) Produced crackle glass from 1966-1987
2) Kept individual glass blowing styles and shapes of each company
3) Kanawha labels were used on all pieces during the merger. (Therefore, pieces made by Hamon would have Hamon characteristics during 1969-1980, although they would carry a Kanawha label during these years.)
4) Colors: Same as the colors listed under the individual companies

Pilgrim produced:
1) Mainly crackle glass from 1950-1970
2) Only fine crackles
3) Only free form hand blown methods
4) Bottoms that had pontil marks (Their pontil marks were not very smooth or finished in most instances.)
5) Colors: amber, blue, three shades of green, ruby, orange, green, brown, purple, crystal, gray, and amberina
6) Many small window sill pieces
7) Very delicate and pulled handles
8) Colored handles prior to the early 1960s
9) Lots of crystal handles—these were produced after 1960

10) Variety of crystal handles that are decorative and unusual
11) Has changed the style of the manufacturer's labels over the years:
    1. Yellow (Oldest label)
    2. Black
    3. White and silver
    4. Black, red, and white
    5. Black, blue, and white
    6. Black and white
12) Two distinct marks on some pieces made by touching a file to the bottom before it had cooled
    a. one looks like "measle marks"
    b. the other looks like "water waves"

Rainbow produced:
1) Crackle glass from late 1950s until 1980
2) Small and medium crackles
3) Mold blown pieces
4) All pieces have pontil mark
5) Pontil marks that were sandblasted leaving the bottom smooth and finished, except for the very early years
6) Large "Paul Revere hat" shaped mouth on pitchers
7) All handles are colored except for ruby red pieces
8) Most all ruby pieces have a crystal handle
9) Three labels:
    a. Older label looks like an opened fan, black and silver, with Rainbow written across the fan
    b. Later years a black and silver bubble shape was used with Rainbow written across it
    c. The bubble style was used in red for seconds that were to be sent to the Rainbow retail store
10) Stoppers with superb craftsmanship...sometimes stoppers would measure longer than the actual piece itself
11) Some painted pieces

Williamsburg produced:
1) Crackled glass from 1971 until around 1974
2) Used Kanawha molds and techniques of crackling
3) Mold blown pieces
4) Only smooth bottoms
5) Colors: All colors produced by Kanawha

Please note that all of the above companies produced "other colors" for promotional purposes and/or special lines. The colors listed here are those used on a regular basis.

5. Specialty Collections

A specialty collector is someone who specializes in one specific area. The specialty collections referred to in this book are kitchen and household collectibles and perfume bottles, but there are many others. Specialty collecting is fun and in most cases, years down the road, it will even pay off.

Kitchen and household collectibles are items found in your kitchen and home...tea pitchers, glasses, salt and pepper shakers, bowls and candy dishes, cruets, and lighting items. Some people collect only salt and pepper shakers while others collect cookie jars, and so on. This type of collecting can save you money while enjoying the hunt. A specialty collector will wait on the most unusual and unique pieces that will enhance his or her collection.

Kitchen and Household Collectibles

Kitchen collectibles can be any item you might find in the kitchen. Represented Front, L-R: Rainbow, Kanawha, two Pilgrim, Kanawha, and Rainbow; Back: Pilgrim.

Kitchen collectibles are very popular with crackle glass collectors. Represented Front, L-R: Unknown, Blenko, Unknown, Rainbow, and Pilgrim; Back, L-R: Unknown and Fry.

Tea and Juice Pitchers

Gray #51 Pilgrim tea pitcher, 1949-1959, H. 12". *Courtesy of Jane and Donald Thompson.* Value $50-$75.

Green #939 Blenko tea pitcher, 1947-1960s, designed by Winslow Anderson, H. 13.5". *Courtesy of Dana Noggle.* Value $75-$100.

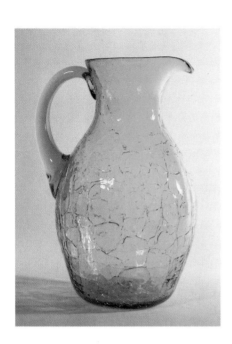

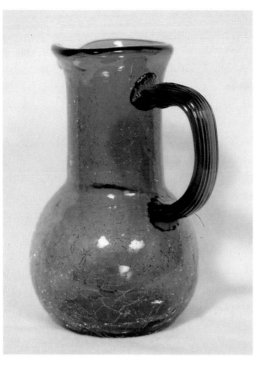

Chartreuse #623 Blenko tea pitcher, 1950s, H. 10.25". *Courtesy of Jane and Donald Thompson.* Value $75-$100.

Brown unidentified tea pitcher with ribbed handle, H. 8". Value $40-$50.

Red Amberina unidentified tea pitcher, H. 11". Value $75-$100.

Tea and juice pitchers are very collectible. Represented L-R: Blenko and three unidentified pitchers.

Orange/amber unidentified tea pitcher, H. 10.5". Value $75-$100.

Crystal unidentified tea pitcher, H. 12". Value $75-$100.

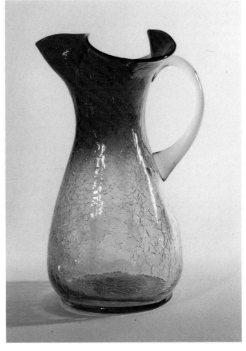

Amberina #88 Kanawha juice pitcher, 1966, H. 9". Value $50-$75.

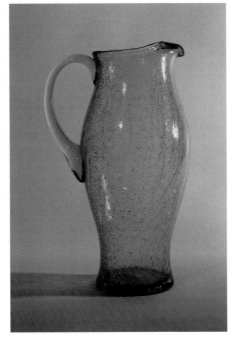

Amber unidentified tea pitcher, H. 11.5". Value $75-$100.

Two-tone dark brown to light green unidentified juice pitcher, H. 8". *Courtesy of Jane and Donald Thompson.* Value $50-$75.

Amberina #85 Kanawha juice pitcher, 1966, H. 13". Value $40-$50.

Ruby red Blenko juice pitcher, 1940s, H. 6.25". Value $50-$75.

Ruby red #361 Bischoff juice pitcher, H. 5.5". Value $50-$75.

Glasses

Olive green Pilgrim pinched glasses, set of eight in carrying case, H. 6". *Courtesy of Jane and Donald Thompson.* Value $175-$225.

Clear unidentified stemmed glass, H. 7.5". *Courtesy of Jane and Donald Thompson.* Value $25-$30.

Clear crystal Blenko glasses with applied rosettes. H. 5.25". Value $50-$75 (set).

A wide variety of crackle glasses are not rare although very collectible.

Two light blue Blenko pinched glasses, H. 5.5". *Courtesy of Jane and Donald Thompson.* Value $40-$50 (pair).

Dark amethyst #7 Kanawha pinched glass, very rare color, 1958-1987, H. 5.5". Value $35-$45.

Clear unidentified pinched shot glasses, set of six, H. 6". Value $50-$75 (set).

Light blue Pilgrim pinched glass, H. 5.75". *Courtesy of Jane and Donald Thompson.* Value $20-$25.

Clear unidentified water glasses, set of six, H. 4.5" Value $100-$150.

Two amber unidentified tea glasses, were bought with the Fry tea pitcher, H. 5.25". Value $40-$50 (set).

Amberina Pilgrim lemonade glasses, set of four, marked, 1949-1969, H. 7.25". *Courtesy of Jane and Donald Thompson.* Value $130-$160.

Amber Pilgrim tea glass with clear foot, 1949-1969, H. 7". *Courtesy of Dana Noggle.* Value $30-$35.

Peach Rainbow stemmed glasses, set of four, 1954-1973, H. 6", $120-$170 (set).

Clear footed unidentified glass, H. 4". Value $20-$25.

Dark amber Blenko pinched tea glasses, set of four, 1949-1969, H. 5.5". Value $75-$100 (set).

Salt and Pepper shakers come in all shapes and sizes.

Clear unidentified salt and pepper shakers with copper tops, H. 3.25". *Courtesy of Jane and Donald Thompson.* Value $25-$35 (set).

Clear unidentified salt and pepper shakers with silver tops, H. 3.25". *Courtesy of Dana Noggle.* Value $20-$25 (set).

Blue #22 Kanawha salt shaker, 1966, H. 7". *Courtesy of Jane and Donald Thompson.* Value $20-$25.

Clear unidentified salt and pepper shakers with plastic tops, H. 2.75". *Courtesy of Dana Noggle.* Value $15-$20 (set).

Crackle glass bowls and candy dishes are found in a variety of colors and shapes.

Decorative candy dishes are very collectible.

Red Pilgrim footed bowl, 1949-1969, 5.5 x 8.5". Value $40-$50.

Green Pilgrim footed bowl, 1949-1969, 5.5 x 8.5". *Courtesy of Jane and Donald Thompson.* Value $35-$45.

Yellow/orange Pilgrim bowl, 1949-1969, 4.25 x 8.5". *Courtesy of Dana Noggle.* Value $30-$40.

Gray Pilgrim candy dish, 1949-1969, 2 x 5.5". Value $20-$25.

Clear Pilgrim bowl, marked, 1949-1969, 3.75 x 8". *Courtesy of Dana Noggle.* Value $30-$40.

Amberina #3744 Blenko bowl, 4.25 x 10". *Courtesy of Jane and Donald Thompson.* Value $35-$45.

Olive green #3744 Blenko bowl, 4.25 x 10". *Courtesy of Jane and Donald Thompson.* Value $30-$40.

Green Blenko footed bowl, 1930-1950, 6 x 5". *Courtesy of Jane and Donald Thompson.* Value $35-$45.

Clear, probably Bischoff bowl, H. 3.25". *Courtesy of Jane and Donald Thompson.* Value $20-$25.

Amberina #154 Kanawha candy dish, 1966, 2 x 5.5". Value $20-$25.

Kanawha oil and vinegar decanters come in a variety of colors, 1966. Represented green, brown, amberina, and purple.

Two Green #112 Pilgrim oil and vinegar cruets, 1959-1969, H. 6", B. 4.5", T. 2.5". *Courtesy of Dana Noggle.* Value $80-$100 (set).

Two Amberina #112 Pilgrim oil and vinegar cruets (one stopper is missing), 1959-1969, H. 6", B. 4.5", T. 2.5". Value $60-$80 (set).

Two Amberina #21 Kanawha oil and
vinegar cruets, 1966, H. 6" A gift from
my children for Mother's Day, 1996.
Value—priceless to mom—$80-$100 (set).

Green #21 Kanawha oil and vinegar
decanter, with silver corked stopper,
1966, H. 6". Value $35-$45.

(Although Sloan Glass Company made many lighting products, I am uncertain of the positive identification for these items.)

Amber hanging light. *Courtesy of Jane and Donald Thompson.* Value $50-$75.

Amber hanging light, H. 23". *Courtesy of Dana Noggle.* Value $50-$75.

Amber craquel globes, H. 6". *Courtesy of Jane and Donald Thompson,* $30-$40 (set).

Amber craquel globe. *Courtesy of Jane and Donald Thompson.* Value $15-$20.

Amber and brass candle holder. *Courtesy of Jane and Donald Thompson.* Value $35-$45.

Perfume Bottles

Perfume bottles are in a class all of their own. All perfume bottles, including crackle glass, are made all over the world, and so their creators are not as easily detected as are the kitchen and household collectibles. Perfume bottles are very popular with the collectors, as some of these items are magnificently decorated with minute detail in each specimen. Look carefully at the display of perfume bottles in this chapter...and notice the detail.

Gold (painted on the inside of the bottle) perfume bottle with decorative Devilbiss atomizer. The top is gorgeous with a dark pink stone for the center, surrounded by tiny pearls. The original box adds value to the piece. H. 3.5". *Courtesy of Jane and Donald Thompson.* Value $75-$100 with box.

Perfume bottles from L-R: satin, iridescent, and painted glass finish are just a few of the wide variety of crackle glass perfume bottles that can be found.

The most collectible of all the Household Specialty Collecting is the Perfume Bottles. Their manufacturers are wide spread.

New clear perfume bottle from Taiwan still in the box with funnel, "Mon image by Paris presents," is written on the box, H. 4.25". *Courtesy of Dana Noggle.* Value $15-$20.

Two very old ice blue and pale pink unidentified perfume bottles with detailed and decorative atomizers. The inside of the bottle is painted silver. The tops are decorated with embossed tulips around the center, with the center being an ice blue and pale pink stone the size of a nickel. H. 4.5". Value $100-$150 (set).

Perfume bottles are a class of their own. Crackle glass perfume bottles are manufactured by a wide variety of companies. Many perfume bottles are manufactured by companies outside the U.S. Many European and, more recently, Taiwan companies import perfume bottles. Represented L-R: Fairly new, brand new, and very old.

Cream colored swirled perfume bottle with decorative atomizer. The tiny top has a painted pink rose with green leaves. The bottom reads Irice, NY #4. H. 3.25". *Courtesy of Jane and Donald Thompson.* Value $40-$50.

Pale pink unidentified perfume bottle, H. 3.5". *Courtesy of Jane and Donald Thompson.* Value $25-$35.

Green unidentified perfume bottle, H. 4". *Courtesy of Dana Noggle.* Value $20-$25.

Dark amethyst unidentified perfume bottle with missing stopper, H. 4". *Courtesy of Jane and Donald Thompson.* Value $40-$50.

Green unidentified perfume bottle, H. 3.5". *Courtesy of Dana Noggle.* Value $20-$25.

Green unidentified perfume bottle with crackled stopper, H. 5.25", B. 3.5", T. 2.5". *Courtesy of Dana Noggle.* Value $25-$35.

Emerald green bottle with Cobalt blue solid round crackled stopper, new, a gift for my birthday from my friend, Mary George Jester, H. 5", B. 4.25", T. 1.5" Value—priceless to the author—$40-$50.

New pale pink perfume bottle with satin flower stopper and crystal hummingbird on the top, H. 6", B. 3.75", T. 3.25". *Courtesy of Dana Noggle.* Value $35-$45.

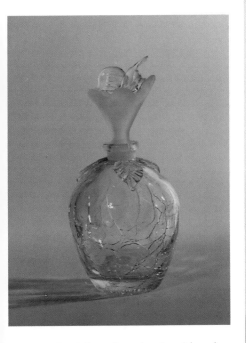

New pale pink perfume bottle with satin flower stopper, crystal hummingbird with head in the satin flower, H. 5", B. 3.5", T. 32.5". *Courtesy of Jane and Donald Thompson.* Value $35-$45.

Bibliography

Books

Eige, Eason and Rick Wilson. *Blenko Glass 1930-1953*. Marietta, Ohio: Antique Publication, 1987.

Fry, H.C. Glass Society. *The Collector's Encyclopedia of Fry Glass*.

Husfloen, Kyle. *The Antique Trader, Antiques and Collectibles Price Guide*. Dubuque, Iowa: The Babka Publishing Company, Sixth Edition, 1990.

Huxford, Sharon and Bob. *Shroeder's Antiques Price Guide*. Paducah, Kentucky: Collector's Books, Thirteenth Edition, 1995.

Piña, Leslie. *Popular 50s And 60s Glass, Color Along the River*. Atglen, Pennsylvania, Schiffer Publishing Ltd., 1995.

Kovel, Ralph and Terry. *Kovel's Antiques and Collectible Price List*. New York, New York: Crown Trade Paperbacks, 1995, 1994, and 1992.

Murphy, Catherine and Kyle Husfloen. *The Antique Trader, Antiques And Collectibles Price Guide*. Dubuque, Iowa: The Babka Publishing Company, Fourth Edition, 1988.

Six, Dean. *The Index to Dean Six's Encyclopedia of West Virginia Glass*. Typescript, 1993.

Weatherman, Hazel Marie. *Colored Glassware of The Depression Era 2*, Springfield, Missouri: Glass Books, 1974.

Weitman, Stan and Arlene. *Crackle Glass, Identification and Value Guide*. Paducah, Kentucky: Collector Books, 1995.

Digest Articles

Linn, Alan. "The Fenton Story." *Glass Collector's Digest*, August/September, 71-78.

McKeand, Robert G. and Thomas O'Conner. "A Formula for Success, The Pilgrim Story." *Glass Collector's Digest*, Volume IV, Number 3, October/November, 1990.

Newspaper Articles

Haworth, James R. "This Is Huntington Rainbow Art Glass Company." *The Huntington Advertiser*, Huntington, West Virginia, November 24, 1956.

Rose, Mara. "Morning Blaze Levels Viking Glass Building." *The Herald Advertiser*, Huntington, West Virginia, 1983.

Sedgwick, Tod. "Viking Glass Here Modernizing Plant." *The Herald Advertiser*, Huntington, West Virginia, August 5, 1973.

Catalogs

Bischoff because it belongs...handcrafted glassware, A.F. Bischoff Glass, Inc., Culloden, West Virginia.

Fenton Catalog, Crackle Glass, 1992, 16-17.

Fenton Catalog, Crackle Glass, 1993, 20-21.

Kanawha Glass Company, Dunbar, West Virginia, 1966 Catalog.

Kanawha Glass Company, Dunbar, West Virginia, 1973 Catalog.

Kanawha Glass Company, Dunbar, West Virginia, 1978 Catalog.

Kanawha Glass Company, Dunbar, West Virginia, Kanawha Glass Catalog, Number 31.

Pilgrim Hand craft Glassware, The Pilgrim Glass Corporation Catalog, Ceredo, West Virginia, U.S.A., 1949-1973.

R - it's Made By Hand, The Rainbow Art Glass Company, Inc., 1968, Division of Viking Glass Company, New Martinsville, West Virginia.

Rainbow Art Glass Catalog Supplement, Handblown Colored Glassware, The Rainbow Art Glass Company, 1965.

Pamphlets

"The Creation of Fine Handblown Glassware by Rainbow," The Rainbow Art Glass Company.

"The Rainbow Handblown Glass...see it created at Rainbow," The Rainbow Art Glass Company.

Personal Interviews

Henry And Emmy Manus, April 1996

Paul Kilgore, April 1996

Robert Hamon, April 1996

Charles T. Sloan, April 1996

Robert McKeand, April 1996

Jack Dereume, June 1996

Keith Merritt, June 1996

Note from the Author

Author's Note:
My Special Love For Crackle Glass

A piece of crackle glass radiates with beauty, especially when it is exposed to the sun. Its beauty is magnified as the sun rays hit the brilliant colors of crackled pieces and bounce off each tiny piece of crackle to expose a brilliant piece of art...to me the sight is breath-taking.

I draw special meaning from this glass because of a story I was told about crackle glass years ago. Crackle glass was invented because of imperfections or flaws in a piece of regular glass. Almost all manufacturers of glass adopted this procedure to save a piece of art work that was blemished or imperfect and would otherwise be tossed out as a loss. Instead of taking a loss due to imperfection the glass maker would crackle the glass and cover up the blemishes or mistakes, and thus we have the birth of crackle glass.

This act reminds me of the story of Christ. We as human beings are blemished and imperfect...but as a Christian, I believe that we are changed by having Christ in our lives. Our imperfections are covered by the blood of Christ who died to save us. God no longer sees our imperfections and blemishes. We are no longer a loss for our creator. Thus we have the birth of Christians.

As the sun shines and radiates the beauty of crackle glass, so the Son shines and radiates His good in us—His people. Both crackle glass and Christians come from blemishes and imperfect products. The blemishes are still there. The only difference is the products were changed and covered...one by crackles and the other by Christ. Thus both are saved, and both now have value.

Index